COMFORT
from
BEYOND

Foreword by DON PIPER

New York Times best-selling author of *90 Minutes in Heaven*

COMFORT

=== *from* ===

BEYOND

*Real-Life Experiences of Hope
in the Face of Loss*

Edited By EVELYN BENCE

New York, New York

Comfort from Beyond

ISBN-13: 978-0-8249-4741-5

Published by Guideposts
16 East 34th Street
New York, New York 10016
www.guideposts.com

Distributed by Ideals Publications, a Guideposts company
535 Metroplex Drive, Suite 250
Nashville, Tennessee 37211

Guideposts and Ideals are registered trademarks of Guideposts.

Acknowledgments

Every attempt has been made to credit the sources of copyrighted material used in this book. If any such acknowledgment has been inadvertently omitted or miscredited, receipt of such information would be appreciated.

All material that originally appeared in *Angels on Earth, Daily Guideposts, Guideposts* and the *Comfort from Beyond* series is reprinted with permission.

"A Book about Bears" and "Purple" by Lonnie Hull DuPont
are used by permission of the author.

"A Golden Gift," originally titled "Listen to the Voice inside Your Head,"
by Patricia Lorenz is used by permission of the author.

"Bonnie" by Betty R. Graham is used by permission of the author.

"Hope and Heaven" by Sharon Betters is from the book *Treasures in Darkness: A Grieving Mother Shares Her Heart*. Used by permission of P&R Publishing, PO Box 817, Phillipsburg, NJ 08865.

"Jesus Has a Rocking Chair" by Kathe Wunnenberg is from the book *Grieving the Child I Never Knew*. Used by permission of Zondervan, 5300 Patterson Ave. SE., Grand Rapids, MI 49530.

Scripture quotations marked (KJV) are taken from *The King James Version of the Bible.*

Scripture quotations marked (NIV) are taken from *The Holy Bible, New International Version.* Copyright © 1973, 1978, 1984 International Bible Society. Used by permission of Zondervan Bible Publishers.

Scripture quotations marked (NKJV) are taken from *The Holy Bible, New King James Version.* Copyright © 1997, 1990, 1985, 1983 by Thomas Nelson, Inc.

Library of Congress Cataloging-in-Publication Data

Comfort from beyond.
   p. cm.
ISBN-13:978-0-8249-4741-5
1. Consolation. I. Guideposts Associates.
BV4905.5.C655 2008
   242'.4—dc22
                    2008005863

Edited by Evelyn Bence
Cover design by Kirk DouPonce, www.DogEaredDesign.com
Interior design by José Fonfrias
Typeset by Nancy Tardi

Printed and bound in the United States of America
10 9 8 7 6 5 4 3 2 1

Contents

Contents

Contents

Contents

Foreword

WHEN MY MOM CALLED ME and my two brothers in from summer play in 1963, we knew something was up. At first we thought her swollen eyes and tear-stained face were reminders that my career–US Army dad had just been deployed to Korea. But this impromptu meeting wasn't about my dad; it was about my dad's mom. Mom told us my Grandma Piper had just died. Tears streamed down our faces. We were ill-equipped to deal with such startling news.

In the following two days I am not sure which disturbed us the most: the funeral of my grandmother or the fact that her son, my dad, was unable to attend his own mother's funeral because he was on a troop ship in the Pacific Ocean.

This being my first encounter with death, my thirteen-year-old mind had trouble dealing with the realization that Grandma Piper was gone. Sure, I'd seen movies, TV shows, even cartoons, where death was portrayed, but this was real. This was my family. As shocking as this revelation was, an even more arresting one awaited me during her funeral in the little white clapboard church: "If Grandma died, then one day I will too!"

Suddenly confronted with my own mortality, I began to struggle with personal loss and heartbreak. I started asking questions about what happens after we die. I wanted to know how I would live now without someone I loved.

Little did I know that twenty-five years later on a rain-slicked Texas highway, those questions would be answered for me. In 1989 I was killed in a car crash and was highly blessed to experience the joy and majesty of heaven, only to be returned to earth to undergo thirty-four surgeries and three years of harrowing rehabilitation and recovery. If I had only had a book like *Comfort from Beyond* during those dark days!

In your hands you hold an excellent resource for encouragement and solace. Weaving a golden thread through these wonderfully uplifting and deeply personal stories are the Psalms. One Psalm in particular describes this book: "He opened the rock and water gushed out. It ran in dry places like a river" (Psalm 105:40). These poignant stories will quench any thirst for hope and inspiration.

As you read each chapter, you will know that angels are real. That God answers prayer. That forgiveness is possible. That grief can be overcome. That heaven is real. And praise God, there is comfort even when there are no answers.

I know. I have experienced all this myself. And now, as you read these pages, you will too.

Don Piper
Author of *90 Minutes in Heaven*

Introduction

Oh, that my words were written!

Job 19:23 NKJV

ON ANY GIVEN SUNDAY, Christians in many liturgical churches, including mine, hear Scripture passages that are previously selected or "appointed" for the day. This morning I happened to look ahead to next Sunday's readings. What a surprise to discover that the Old Testament excerpt starts with these exclamations of suffering Job. He had a wish—to write his story. But the very next verse indicates that Job wanted the world to know about something bigger than his present physical or emotional pain. He wanted to turn his readers' attention to his God and to the hope of life beyond death. The passage continues:

> For I know that my Redeemer lives . . .
> And after my skin is destroyed, this I know,
> That in my flesh I shall see God.
> Whom I shall see for myself,
> And my eyes shall behold, and not another. (vv. 24–27)

I smiled at God's timing. I've spent weeks compiling, honing, and shaping this book. I feel as if I've been walking along with dozens of men and women in the long valley of the shadow of death. And then, the very day I intend to write the introduction, I discover this ancient declaration that mirrors the motivation of so many of the writers included in this selection. They mourn the loss of loved ones. They know grief's pain. But in their distress they look to God for comfort, and, like Job, they boldly share their stories of God's faithful presence. They claim the assurance that there is life after death. What's more, they have become confident that their departed family members or friends are among the heavenly company of witnesses watching down on them with tender care.

In *Comfort from Beyond*, dozens of contributors reveal the striking—or sometimes subtle—ways God has used to reveal the truth of Jesus' promise in John 14:18 KJV: "I will not leave you comfortless." Some have seen angels at a deathbed, whisking a soul away. Some have had extended conversations with people who appear for a while and then vanish, leaving behind little more than a healed heart. Some have seen visions that calmed their fears or dreamt scenes that eased their griefs. Some sense that nature—a flower, a pet, a wild bird—has relayed a message from a deceased loved one; signs and symbols, sights and sounds, speak comfort: *I'm all right. I haven't forgotten you. I'll see you again.*

If you have lost someone you love—a child, a spouse, a parent, a friend—you'll want to keep this collection of true stories at your bedside, by your recliner, on your breakfast table or in your car. It's a book to "dip into," reading a few stories or a section at a sitting, whether you're looking for a reason for hope; an example of the power of God to answer prayer; a nudge that will help you take a step toward forgiving someone responsible for your loss; assurance that God has a purpose and direction for the remainder of your days.

We're confident that, over a period of time, you'll be strengthened in spirit, renewed with strength, comforted within—from beyond.

Each thematic section opens with words from a psalm, words that remind us that we are not alone in our sorrows and in our discoveries of grace. King David and other ancient poets, like Job, wrote out their emotions and recorded their attempts to reach out for God, even as God reached out for them. As a result of reading, maybe you'll similarly be inspired to write—to journal—an account of your own journey through grief, as you learn to savor positive memories and walk in and with the hope of an earthly life worth living and an eternal life in the heavenly hereafter.

PART I

Answers to Prayer

Give ear to my prayer, O God,
And do not hide Yourself from my supplication.
Attend to me, and hear me;
I am restless in my complaint . . . .
My heart is severely pained within me,
And the terrors of death have fallen upon me.

Psalm 55:1–2, 4 NKJV

WHEN WE ARE OVERWHELMED BY GRIEF, our days and nights can feel like one long anguished prayer for God's help. That's the heart-prayer of the psalmist: "Give ear to my prayer, O God. . . . I am restless in my complaint." It's the prayer I see in Frank Bianco's story. When visiting a monastery on a work assignment, Frank unexpectedly found peace that he hardly knew he was asking for.

But there are other forms of prayer. Most of the personal stories selected for this section show specific answers to specific requests for comfort, healing, assurance. As Steve Kelley admits at the beginning of "A Baseball Promise," it's hard to believe that God would turn His ear toward a young child's prayer over a baseball game, and yet he later acknowledges his lesson, that we can talk to God "even about baseball." Keep reading, and you'll find Cynthia Roberts describing a vision in which she sees the prayers of family and friends as "a chain of lights" she needs to reach toward. May that image encourage you to reach out to receive the grace God grants you today.

A Baseball Promise

by Steve Kelley

A S SOON AS THE WORDS were out of my mouth, I would have given anything to take them back.

I looked at that youngster beside me in the car, pixie face eager beneath her baseball cap. Knowing just how much ten-year-old Erin missed her dad, and wanting to do something special for her, I'd invited her to go with me that afternoon to watch the Giants play the Chicago Cubs at Candlestick Park. I'd never seen a kid so excited. We'd been driving across the Bay Bridge when she suddenly piped up, "Maybe we'll catch a foul ball!"

And like an idiot I'd said, "Well, honey, now that your dad's in heaven, maybe he'll mention that to God for you."

Just a throwaway remark, but I saw that she took it seriously, and I wanted to bite my tongue off. A child's faith is tested enough when a parent dies without some dolt planting pipe dreams.

"You mean," Erin asked in an awestruck voice, "you can talk to God even about baseball?"

I switched subjects fast, talked about some of the great times our two families had had together. We were like one family, really, next-door neighbors for eleven years, each couple with three kids the same ages, and Craig and I as close as brothers in spite of being so different.

It was our differences, in fact, that made the relationship so great. Craig could repair anything—electrical circuits, clogged plumbing. When my kids had a bike wheel come off, they wouldn't waste time with me; they'd go straight to him.

As for me, sports were my thing, especially baseball. I'd gone to college on a baseball scholarship, been drafted by the California Angels to a minor-league contract right out of school. After four years I was aspiring to a spot in the major leagues when I damaged my rotator cuff. That ended my professional career, but not my love of the game. We made a deal, Craig and I: Things that needed fixing, he'd do; coaching the kids was my job.

All six of them were great little athletes, but Erin was something else. Lots of speed, a pitcher's concentration and a throwing arm every guy in her Little League division envied. (She played on a boys' team.) It made a special bond between the two of us, all the more important in the six months since her dad's death from Hodgkin's lymphoma.

I'd never forget his final words to me in the hospital room a few hours before the end. "Keep a watch over my kids, Steve." As if he had to ask!

As we pulled into the parking lot at Candlestick, Erin chattered away, my thoughtless remark forgotten, I hoped.

Soon we were settled into our seats halfway between home plate and third base, Cracker Jack boxes in hand. The pitcher warmed up, and we prepared for our private contest. When I first started taking kids to ball games, I'd invented a way to pass the slow moments between pitches. Each of us would call out a guess as to what would happen. "High pop-up to right field!" Or, "Line drive to center!"

Ninety-nine percent of the guesses were wrong, of course, but when someone did predict correctly, he or she got a point toward an extra hot dog or a souvenir program. Erin was calling, "Swing and a miss on a curve ball!" unfazed by a score of zero.

It was a wonderful afternoon, a close game with some spectacular plays. Like the baseball fanatics we were, we'd both brought our mitts, though Erin—to my vast relief—hadn't spoken again about a foul ball coming our way, the notion apparently forgotten as quickly as it came.

It was in the bottom of the ninth, game nearly over with two outs and the batter up, that she stood up suddenly and sang out, "High foul ball right to us!"

I laughed at the certainty with which she could still make these pronouncements. There was a crack as the batter connected with the ball, sending it high over the third-base line. A second later the laughter died in my throat as I watched the trajectory of that ball, saw it spin, curve to the left, and begin a slow downward arc right toward us.

All around us people were on their feet, arms raised,

grabbing for it. I'm a tall guy, six-foot-five. I leaned forward and stretched my hand up. The ball slapped into the fingertips of my mitt.

Erin was jumping, laughing, crying, brushing away tears with her own mitt. I started crying too, the two of us shouting, hugging each other, staring at that miraculous ball. Erin looked at the ball, that is. I was seeing something more wondrous still. I was watching a child's first encounter with the God we can talk to even about baseball.

Chain of Lights

by Cynthia Roberts

TIRED . . . TIRED ALL THE TIME. For a whole year it had been a struggle just to drag myself out of bed. But I had to. Besides the house and a very sick husband to take care of, there was my job as caretaker for a bedridden lady.

So I kept going through fall and winter. Through the spring, through June and July. People needed me, and I loved being needed! When my husband David was diagnosed with terminal cancer, he worried about becoming a burden, but I didn't see it that way at all. Caring for him would be a privilege.

Family and friends offered to pitch in, but I waved them away. I had always looked after people. Neighbors, children, anyone I could help. As a teenager I stayed with elderly neighbors, people who otherwise would have had to move out of their houses. After I was married, even as our five children came along, I went out and cared for people in their homes. The income was welcome, of course, but more important to me was knowing I was needed.

So, even after the strange tiredness began, I wouldn't slow down. Wouldn't accept a neighbor's offer to run errands. Wouldn't let a friend bring in a meal. Wouldn't admit I couldn't do everything myself—even when lifting a sack of groceries from the car left me gasping for breath.

On August 6, my daughter and her husband dropped by for a visit, took one look at me and announced they were taking me straight to Nantucket Cottage Hospital. I was so weak my son-in-law had to carry me out to the car. Even so, I wouldn't let them put me in a hospital bed till they assured me their dad would be well cared for.

The last thing I remember is holding the bedside telephone, speaking to my sister. I'm told that a nurse, entering the room a little later, found me with the phone in my hand, asleep. She was unable to wake me. I have no memory of the battle around that bed to save my life, the emergency intubation, the medivac airlift from the island to the New England Medical Center in Boston. Of that entire week I remember nothing at all, and of the days after that I recall only fragmentary dreamlike impressions of being in a hospital room with doctors and nurses and family members coming and going.

The eventual diagnosis was babesiosis, a sometimes-fatal tick-borne infection. In the year that it had gone untreated, no part of my system had escaped damage. Lungs, heart, kidneys. . . . I'm told my arms and legs swelled to almost twice their normal size.

Why I had failed to seek help for my constant tiredness was a mystery to the doctors—but no mystery to people like me who've always been the help givers. I had needed help, desperately, and now, medically speaking, it was too late.

I was aware of none of that. I knew only I was cold, so cold. . . .

And it was then, as I lay in a cold gray limbo where my mind groped among shadows, that I saw, suspended in the air before me, perhaps two feet away, a chain of warm, softly glowing lights. Each light stood out distinctly, red with some inner heat, like a burning coal, separate—yet somehow linked with the others. Without a moment's doubt I knew what those glowing lights were and why they were there. They were prayers. The prayers of other people. For me!

I stared at the lights, overwhelmed. Were others at that moment supporting me when I could do nothing for myself? The lights were so warm, and I was so cold! I wanted that warmth closer still, enfolding me.

I knew it was the moment of decision. I knew the lights could come no closer until I asked for them. I had to reach out, receive the gift. In my mind—because of the tube in my throat I'm sure I didn't speak aloud—I said, I accept them.

I reached out my hands (again in my mind) and drew the shining vision toward me. I wrapped those lights about my shoulders like a shawl, feeling their warmth, their comfort, their healing.

And I began to heal from that moment on. New England Medical Center is a teaching hospital. Dr. Jeffrey Gelfand led a marveling troop of interns through my room each day as my strength returned. When I was discharged from the medical center on August 28, he told me I was the sickest patient ever admitted with that kind of illness to leave alive.

At home I began to learn the details of the prayers I had seen in the lights above my bed. Friends, family, even strangers, had mounted a prayer campaign. Not only my own church but other churches on the island were praying for me. So much love, so much caring . . . for me.

My physical healing was a miracle, but to me the spiritual healing was just as miraculous. After a lifetime of giving, I had learned to do what for many of us is far harder: I had learned to receive. To receive the prayers that changed my life. To take the helping hand stretched out in love.

Why is that so difficult? Is it pride? Self-sufficiency? The idea that we can somehow earn acceptance by other people—by God—if we "do" enough?

Oh, there's been plenty to do for others during the years since. For one, I'm so grateful I was able to care for David during the final months of his life. But these past years have been filled with another kind of joy as well. The joy of being able at last to speak three little words aloud: "I need you."

Herbie's Purr

by Ruth McDaniel

CRATCH, SCRATCH. . . .

I looked up from the insurance form I was trying to fill out and glanced toward the kitchen. Could that be what I thought it was? No, that's impossible. It sounded just like a paw softly scratching the screen door—something I hadn't heard since Fluffy, our cat of twenty years, had died.

Fluffy had wandered into our lives, a stray. "She looks like she's been living off the land for a while now," my husband W.T. said as we watched her stealthily creep along the border of our backyard early one evening. She was clearly looking for food, but the second we opened the door, she shot back into the woods.

"The poor thing," I said as the cat peeked out at us from among the leaves. "She's afraid of people. Too wary for her own good."

"She'll come around," W.T. said. "She just needs some time to learn to trust us."

Every evening when he got home from work, W.T. went straight out back with a bowl of milk or food. Finally the day came when he was able to stroke the cat's yellow fur once before she scampered back to the safety of the woods. "She's so fluffy!" he marveled. So that was how Fluffy came to have her name. For the next twenty years, though she was a beloved pet, she always retained that little spark of wildness and independence.

When Fluffy passed away, W.T. was heartbroken. It was a few months afterward that his own health began to decline. Now W.T. was gone too, and I was alone in a house that seemed wonderfully secluded when we'd moved in years back but suddenly felt just plain lonely. And it had only been a week.

Scratch, scratch. . . .

There it is again! Must be a branch rubbing against the window screen.

With W.T. gone, the sensible thing would have been to sell the house and move into a smaller space—one where the nearest neighbor wasn't a mile away. But there were no apartments in town, and I hated the idea of leaving the place where my husband and I had spent so many wonderful years. Plus there were all of W.T.'s possessions to deal with, from his tools and fishing gear to the little outboard he kept on blocks in the carport. Everywhere I looked, there seemed to be another detail to worry about, and another reminder of my grief. *Lord, who is going to help me with all this? How will I get by?*

Scratch, scratch. . . .

Okay, I've got to go see what that noise is. I put the insurance form down and went to the kitchen. I gave a little start when I saw the cat looking at me from behind the screen. *It can't be—but it looks just like Fluffy!* I pushed open the door, and my visitor, purring loudly, strolled right inside and rubbed against my leg. The yellowish color was the same as Fluffy's, but this cat was bigger—clearly a male —and a lot more trusting. Even after twenty years with us, Fluffy would never have just sauntered in like that.

All that thick fur couldn't conceal the cat's emaciated condition, and his meows begged for food. I poured a big bowl of milk, and the cat followed me out to the carport. He lapped up the milk eagerly. I spread out an old blanket in case he decided to stay for the night.

The next morning I called some neighbors and the town veterinarian, asking if anyone had lost a cat. No one had. I plunged into another day of bills, forms and phone calls. In the afternoon, depressed and hardly able to think straight, I went into the kitchen to make myself a cup of coffee.

Scratch, scratch. . . . There was that paw on the screen again.

"I guess you've got yourself a new owner," I said, opening a can of Fluffy's cat food I'd unearthed from the back of the cupboard. I served my new friend and sat down at the kitchen table to watch him eat. When he finished, he came over and hopped in my lap.

"You really are a friendly one! Herbie sounds like a good name for you," I said as I stroked his thick coat. Herbie set to purring that purr of his. Before I knew it, I was beginning to feel myself again, and I even found the energy for a few more phone calls.

From then on, Herbie and I established a routine. Whenever some new bill or legal detail got the better of me, I'd go out back and holler, "Herbie!" There would be a rustle in the woods, and he'd run into the house, hop up onto my lap and start purring. "Relax," the sound always seemed to say. "Things will work out. Just wait and see."

Herbie wasn't the only one giving me encouragement. When a storm blew some heavy branches down into the yard, a few friends from church showed up without my even asking and helped me clear them. One neighbor found a buyer for W.T.'s fishing boat, and another guided me through the confusing details of his insurance papers.

One morning, as I was reading the paper with Herbie curled contentedly in my lap, a friend called to tell me about a condominium that was going up in town. I could move to a more manageable space without leaving the area behind after all. I soon found a buyer for the house, and he agreed to take most of the furniture too. I also discovered that one of the neighbors who had helped me was an avid fisherman. It was a joy to be able to pass on W.T.'s gear to him. "See?" Herbie's purr seemed to say. "I told you so."

But as moving day approached, I found myself with a new worry. Herbie was an outdoor cat. Would he be comfortable in a small apartment? The last thing I wanted was to make him miserable by cooping him up.

Like I always did now when a worry was starting to get the better of me, I went to the kitchen door.

"Herbie! Herrrrbie!"

But for the first time since that big yellow cat had walked into my life, Herbie was nowhere to be seen.

I drove around the countryside and made some calls—to no avail. Worrier though I was, I somehow knew no harm had come to Herbie. When the time was right, he had left just as mysteriously as he had come. I said a prayer for his well-being and promised that when things got tough in the future, I'd remember that soothing purr of his. When I'd really needed it, God's help had been there—right at my screen door.

Heaven's Lamb

by Sue Draper

$\mathcal{S}$AMMY WAS A TEENAGER when he took his first plane trip, but he'd been talking about it long before. Talking about it in his own Sammy way, that is. Deaf and with Down syndrome, my brother communicated with my parents and me by using sign language for the things that were all-important to him—mostly food, like his favorite hamburgers and fries, but also paper and scissors and airplanes.

My brother and I grew up in Los Angeles, and our parents often drove us out to the airport to watch the planes take off. Sammy would put his first finger and pinky out straight and make flying motions with his hand for as long as we would stay. When I got my first job, which involved a great deal of travel, the whole family would come to the airport and see me off.

After one business trip, Sammy wouldn't leave me alone. "Airplane," he signed while I tried to unpack. "I had a wonderful flight, Sammy," I said, sliding my foot into my slipper. My toes hit something, and I reached inside my slipper to see what it was—a magazine cutout of an airplane! That night we found planes under our dinner plates.

Sammy piloted his hand over the serving bowls of mashed potatoes and peas, and then poked his thumbs at his chest. "Understand?" he asked, using one of the few words he could say flawlessly. Sammy wanted to fly.

My parents and I discussed it. I wanted to make Sammy happy. But what if he got frightened in the air? How would I reassure him? Sammy couldn't grasp abstract concepts. We could teach him about love by hugging him, but gravity was beyond his reach. I might as well have tried to explain what heaven was.

Then I heard about a twenty-five-minute flight from LA to San Diego. I figured I could distract him for that long, and if the trip was a disaster, we could return another way. Mom encouraged me. "My instincts say Sammy's up to it," she said. "And you can visit the San Diego Zoo."

I bought two tickets and tried to prepare Sammy for our big adventure. Mom and Dad drove us to the airport and watched us board the plane, Sammy with his backpack full of snacks. *God*, I asked as we settled into our seats, *let this trip be a good memory for Sammy*.

He sat stiff in his seat during takeoff, a bit surprised by the sudden vibration. I distracted him once we were airborne, not sure how he'd take to the feathery whiteness outside. When the flight attendant brought Coke and peanuts, Sammy could hardly contain his excitement, and twenty-five minutes went by without incident—except that Sammy asked "the lady" three more times for extra nuts.

In San Diego, at the zoo, Sammy named all the animals. I couldn't tear him away from the sweet white lambs at the petting zoo. He patted the thick curly fleece on their backs and closed his eyes while one gave him a lick. Sammy balled his hand and crossed his arms over his heart. "I know, Sammy," I said. "You love the lambs, don't you?"

He talked nonstop about the animals until our plane took off for home. Sammy seemed braver on the return flight, pressing his face against the window once we were up in the sky. "Clouds," he signed, making C-shaped hands face each other and moving them slowly to the right. Then he tilted his head and tucked his hands under his cheek. "Yes, Sammy," I said. "The clouds are soft as a pillow. It's very peaceful up here, isn't it? Dreamy and peaceful." The sun was shining bright, and the puffy white clouds were backlit with golden halos. *Can you get any closer to heaven than this?* I wondered. Sammy patted my arm, and we looked out the window together. Our trip couldn't have been more perfect.

Back in LA by late afternoon, Sammy told our parents about the lady with peanuts and the fluffy clouds. Then he put his fingers in a V and made a clipping motion up his forearm, for "lamb."

"I loved the lambs most," he signed, balling his hand and crossing his arms over his chest.

That plane ride seemed to satisfy Sammy's curiosity and forever linked lambs and the clear blue sky in his mind.

Over the next few years he continued to cut out airplanes, and he learned to draw them. When our mother was diagnosed with cancer in 1997, Sammy spent long hours on the floor with his paper next to where she lay on the sofa, drawing airplanes and cutting them out, his offerings to Mom. It was a hard year, with Mom in and out of the hospital, and it broke my heart that I couldn't explain to Sammy that these were her last days. Eventually Mom went into the hospital. She died in November 1998, an airplane under her pillow from the last time Sammy had seen her.

Dad and I decided not to take Sammy to Mom's funeral. Seeing her body in a coffin would frighten him, and we'd never be able to assure him that she was safe in heaven with God. But we were at a loss for words when Sammy asked when she was coming home. He had a picture of Mom he carried with him in his wallet always. He'd pull it out and stare at it, not understanding why another day had passed and we hadn't visited her in the hospital.

One day, while we were out running errands, Sammy waved and blew a kiss as we passed the hospital. *Dear God, how do I make Sammy understand?*

At home Sammy got busy cutting out his paper airplanes, and I sneaked into the living room to sort through old photographs. *Oh, Mom*, I thought, *Dad and I haven't handled this well with Sammy*. I couldn't imagine how we were going to make things right.

I felt a tap on my shoulder and turned from the picture album. Sammy looked at me the way I look at him when I want his undivided attention.

"What is it, Sammy?" I sat down with him and asked.

He pulled out his wallet and flipped it open to the picture of Mom. "Airplane," Sammy signed. "Airplane to the sky."

What do I say now? Did Sammy think Mom had gone off and abandoned him? "Oh, Sammy," I started, tears filling my eyes. But Sammy wasn't upset. Or sad. He was calm, peaceful even. He patted my arm, as if he knew something I didn't. Something for certain. Something I needed to know too.

"Mom is with the lambs," he explained, "in the sky." My brother waited for me to take it in. "Understand?" he asked.

"Yes, Sammy." And I did. God had given Sammy the perfect picture of heaven.

Trying to Remember Michael

by Frank Bianco

Y WIFE MARIE AND I WERE LEAVING for freelance writing assignments in Virginia that June morning. We said good-bye to our youngest son, Michael, who in two weeks would be graduating from high school in Long Island, New York.

Generous, outgoing, always eager to help others, Michael brought sunshine to everyone around him. I looked at his handsome face and rumpled his curly brown hair. Every feature on that face was dear to me.

"Bye, Dad," he said. "Take good care of the camper." I'd promised that as a graduation present he and a classmate could take it on a trip out West. I gave him a bear hug. "So long, Mikey," I said, using his childhood nickname. "Take care of you."

Marie and I reached Monticello, Thomas Jefferson's home in Virginia, and the next morning set off on foot to photograph the sunrise. When we returned, the spot where we'd left the camper was empty. The brakes had somehow failed, and the camper had rolled down a steep abutment.

We were waiting glumly at an auto repair shop when the sheriff walked in. "I've been looking for you folks," he said. "Your family back in New York has been trying to reach you."

Now what? Exasperated, I dialed home. Our twenty-one-year-old son Jimmy picked up the phone on the first ring. "Dad," he said. Why did his voice sound so strange? "Michael's been in an accident."

"What kind of accident? Is he okay?"

"Michael . . ." Jimmy's voice trembled and then broke completely. "He was driving not far from school and skidded on a curve. He hit a truck head-on. He's . . . he's dead."

The days that followed passed in an anguished blur. I tried to comfort Marie, to be a bulwark for the rest of the family. But I was overwhelmed by my own grief. Marie had her faith to keep her going; so did the kids. But I had nothing to which I could cling.

I'd been born and raised a Catholic and had even once studied for the priesthood. But I'd discarded the idea of God as too unsophisticated and irrelevant to apply to my own life. Now, blindsided by this terrible loss, I turned in fury on the Creator my wife believed in. How could a merciful God—any God—exist when my vibrant young son was gone?

At Michael's funeral Mass I knelt next to Marie in the front pew, my son's coffin so close I could have touched it.

The congregation, filled with friends and relatives, raised their voices in a hymn. "You who dwell in the shelter of the Lord . . ."

I felt no shelter, only cold rage. In the days that followed, I numbly returned to my work, carried on my daily duties. And as I did so, I became more and more aware of another devastating dimension of my loss. I couldn't remember Michael.

It wasn't just his body that was gone. My memories of him had disappeared. As the months passed, there were moments when Marie and my other children suddenly brightened. "Remember when Michael had all those hotels stacked up on Park Place?" Jimmy asked once as we played Monopoly, and the others laughed, obviously remembering Michael's facial expressions, gestures, voice.

But I had no such memories to console me. Even staring at photographs of Michael, talking to his friends or handling his possessions resulted in an emotional zero. Not only was my son gone from my life, but all traces of him were gone from my mind as well. I was unable to shed a tear; my bitterness toward God deepened.

The first anniversary of Michael's death came and went. But time, supposedly the great healer, wasn't helping me at all. I still was suffering a strange and cruel sort of amnesia. At night I'd lie in bed trying to see Michael in my mind, to hear his voice, to reexperience and gain solace from the good times we'd had together. I wanted desperately to remember—just remember—Michael. But try as I might, there was nothing. It was as if my son had never existed.

That July, Marie and I drove south once again, this time for story assignments in Kentucky. I had begun to think that suicide would be the only way out of my isolation and despair.

I went through the motions of coping. When Marie and I stopped for coffee in a small Kentucky diner, we chatted with the waitress. "If you're looking for stories," she said, "why don't you drive up the road? There's a Trappist monastery there. The monks support themselves on the food they raise."

"Sounds interesting," Marie said.

"You go," I said. "I'll figure out something else to do."

Anything else. I knew about the Trappists from my days in the seminary. They were considered a spiritual elite, a silent order known for quiet contemplation. They were also known for the most beautiful singing this side of heaven.

Marie's hand was on mine. "Come on," she said gently. "Let's check this place out."

Grudgingly I drove for several miles down a winding country lane toward the Abbey of Gethsemani. It was just after five o'clock when we passed through a wide wooden gate flanked by high white-stuccoed walls.

I parked the car and looked up at the words on the stone arch above the gate. *Pax intrantibus,* meaning, "Peace to all who enter."

Yeah, right. A nice-sounding sentiment for saps who were taken in by that sort of thing. I tramped along behind Marie toward a quadrangle surrounded by unadorned, whitewashed buildings.

On the west side of the quadrangle stood a plain-looking structure whose facade was broken only by a series of narrow stained-glass windows. "That must be the church," Marie said, starting toward it.

The last place I wanted to go was into a church. I started to tell Marie I'd wait outside, but she was already over the threshold. Reluctantly I stepped in too.

The light was dim and the quiet so complete that it almost took my breath away. Something stirred deep inside me, an almost imperceptible trembling. What was I getting into? I followed Marie up the steps at the rear of the church and took a seat in the balcony.

We looked down into a sanctuary built from clay bricks handmade by the abbey's founders more than a hundred years ago. The walls were painted white. The altar was a slab of unadorned gray stone with a simple wooden crucifix hanging beside it.

Below us were perhaps fifty monks in plain woven robes, seated facing each other in rows of wooden choir stalls. There was no talk, no movement, only complete quiet. For the first time in months, perhaps even years, I felt a hush spreading slowly, deeply inside me.

A rap sounded. The monks rose with barely a rustle. Another rap, the signal for the monks to begin.

A shiver went down my spine. As the light streamed in glowing rays across the floor, the voices of the monks swelled and rose as one, offering in majestic cadence words from the Psalms that had been repeated over the centuries. The words were sung carefully, slowly, reverently—and with unwavering conviction and profound intelligence.

Was I shaking? Was the chapel moving? A glowing illumination filled the air. I glanced at Marie. No, she didn't seem to be noticing anything unusual.

But I was stunned by a realization that left no room for doubt. As the monks sang, giving voice to liturgies and prayers that had endured for generations, I knew for a fact: They were talking to someone. And someone was listening. As surely as a baseball pitcher winds up and throws because he knows there is a catcher, these prayers were being sent out, and someone was receiving them.

Then, it was as if a door had been flung open. For the first time since Michael died, memories of my beloved son flooded me. I saw his handsome face as clearly as if he were standing in front of me. I saw him smiling and in my mind heard him speaking as clearly as he had before we left that last day. *It's okay, Dad. It's me, Mikey.*

For more than an hour, as the monks continued to pray and sing, my senses overflowed with my son's presence. I remembered. Scenes of happy times we'd shared over the years replayed in my mind. I was filled with gratitude that I had known him, held him, loved him.

The bells tolled the closing Angelus. And as they did, I heard the words inside me, emanating from a source beyond any earthly comprehension: *I know how it feels. I lost a beloved Son myself. And I love Mikey too, you know.*

Thoughts of taking my own life vanished. I knew that they were gone for good.

I wept. I wept in the arms of God and felt His peace. Peace to all who entered.

PART II

Comfort at Christmas

How shall we sing the Lord's song
In a foreign land?

Psalm 137:4 NKJV

He remembered His holy promise,
And Abraham His servant.
He brought out His people with joy,
His chosen ones with gladness.

Psalm 105:42–43 NKJV

WE CONNECT CHRISTMAS with specific colors: showy red and green, snowy white. When a loved one is absent from the circle, the prevailing hue can be so-sad blue. Who can possibly think of the season or day as a celebration? But you're about to meet some ordinary people—daughters, mothers, widows—who were surprised to find a brighter shade at Christmastime: at the sighting of a particular book, a thoughtful gift, a significant dream, a surprise visitor. Pet owners may especially resonate with "Christmas Morning in the Pasture," about a beloved terrier who wandered away from home one frosty Christmas Eve. Even if it's not Christmastime, these stories can brighten the color of a sad blue heart by adding a tint of joy and gladness—the Christmas promise.

A Book about Bears

by Lonnie Hull DuPont

*M*Y PARENTS DIVORCED when I was small, and from the time I was five years old, my growing up was split in some way between two households. My father, with whom my sister and I spent most weekends, was a complicated man. Emotionally damaged from a troubling childhood, he vacillated between being very sweet or frighteningly angry. And he wasn't great with small children.

Dad's volatile personality made him a distant father during my childhood, and visitations usually ended up with my going to movies all day with my cousins or even by myself. But once I was old enough to drive and had some control over when and how often I saw my father, visitations were not so forced, and things got better between us. Plus, fortunately, Dad was mellowing with age.

I had a car in high school and college, and I would drive to Dad's house whenever I wanted to see him, which became often. We'd have great talks, sometimes long into the night. Away from one another, we would also talk on the phone for hours. Consequently, in my young adult years, my father and I managed to develop a surprising and wonderful relationship. In many ways he was more a friend than a father, and that was okay.

At Christmastime, even in the distant years, Dad had a knack for giving delightful, sometimes extravagant presents. When I was fifteen, I received a small television from him, the smallest I'd ever seen, and it worked for the next twenty years. When personal calculators first hit the market, I received one built into a sturdy checkbook case. When purses that looked like lunch boxes were in vogue, he gave me a lovely one lined in velvet and filled with half dollars.

But I found buying gifts for him to be difficult because he had everything, and what he didn't have, I couldn't afford to buy him. We developed a running ritual as Christmas approached where I would say, "What do you want for Christmas, Daddy?" He would answer in a mock-wistful voice, "Just you." And we'd smile at each other. Fortunately he loved one hundred-percent wool socks for those cold Michigan winters, and I gave those to him every Christmas.

Eventually I left my hometown to pursue a career in book publishing. Because of my love of books, I have always liked giving them as gifts, but I didn't come from a family of readers. Nevertheless, one year I asked my father if there was any kind of book he might want for Christmas. He thought for a moment and then said, "A book about bears." I had no idea my father liked bears. But I rose to the challenge of finding him such a book.

I lived in New York City at the time, a true book town, and I scoured the stores hoping to find a handsome coffee-table book about bears, maybe something from National Geographic. I found no such thing. There were gorgeous, full-color books about all kinds of critters—horses, dogs, cats, reptiles, even creatures from the Great Barrier Reef—but none about bears. Finally one day I found an obscure paperback called *Alaskan Bear Tales*. No photos, no color, only true narratives by people who met up with bears in Alaska and lived to tell about it. I bought the book, added some wool socks, and took those gifts home for Christmas with Dad.

He loved the book. He found the stories riveting, and he told me all about them as he read them. Besides the annual wool socks, this modest book appeared to be the best gift I ever gave him.

A couple of years later, I moved across the country to San Francisco. Three time zones is a long way, and I didn't get to Michigan as often as I'd have liked. One day Dad called me in the middle of the afternoon at my office, something he had never done before. He talked and talked for almost an hour. He told me that when he was a child, he'd almost drowned and that he'd seen the most wonderful things in his mind while he was underwater. He said that ever since then, he'd not been afraid to die. I listened, and I even felt compelled to take notes. Before we said good-bye, we made plans for me to come home in a few weeks for Thanksgiving.

But two weeks before Thanksgiving, Dad died suddenly. He was working outside that morning, pulling a fence post. Then he got into his truck, started it up, and had a massive heart attack with his foot on the accelerator. His neighbor watched the truck roam around the backyard in circles and finally run into a small tree. He hurried to the truck and found my father dead behind the wheel.

At 4:00 AM California time that morning, I woke up suddenly in complete despair and did not know why. I felt as if I'd just had a bad dream, but I couldn't recall actually having had one. I felt horrible, to the point where I started crying. I lived alone then, and I got out of bed and wandered around my apartment, trying to shake this overwhelming feeling of gloom. As I stood in my kitchen, I had the strongest sensation of not being alone. I even peered around in the dark. Then I shook my head, laughed at myself, and went back to bed. I slept peacefully for two more hours until my sister called and said, "I'm afraid I have bad news. . . ."

By the time I got to Michigan, Dad's body had been cremated. There was nothing left of him but ashes. Maybe that's why I had the hardest time believing he was really gone. At his house after the funeral, the neighbor who found him approached me and told me what had happened that day. I asked him what time it was when Dad died, and the neighbor replied, "It was around seven in the morning," which was four in the morning in California. There was no doubt in my mind that my father had come to me as he left this world. I wished that I had realized it at the time and not felt so afraid. Still, I felt comforted.

I began dreaming about my father after that. In the dreams, he would pass through rooms just ahead of me, and I was never able to catch up to him. Or he stood on the other side of a river or a busy highway that I could not cross and watched me with kind eyes. Sometimes he waved to me. He never spoke in these dreams, and I could not touch him, but I had the strongest, sweetest feeling of being in his presence.

I no longer felt compelled to go to Michigan for Christmas. It just wouldn't be the same. Then one day in San Francisco, shortly before my second Christmas without Dad, I walked through my neighborhood on my way to work, and when I passed the used bookstore I passed every single day, in the window, face-out, was a book that had never been there before: a faded copy of *Alaskan Bear Tales*.

Of course I bought it. I still have it. I consider it my perennial Christmas gift from Dad.

One More Visit

by Kathryn Hillis

Y THREE-YEAR-OLD SON KENNY held tight to my hand as he released a red balloon into the chill air that Christmas afternoon. "Do you think Jesus will like His birthday gift, Mommy?" he asked.

"I'm sure of it, darling," I said, squeezing his hand. As I watched the balloon drift up into the sky, I asked, *Please, God, don't take Kenny from me—not yet.* My son had been born with a serious heart defect. He'd already had two heart attacks, and the doctors told me he probably wouldn't make it past the age of five. Some days I prayed for a miracle cure. Others, when Kenny's lips turned blue just from the exertion of climbing into my lap, I held him close and simply prayed for more time. Another month, another year—another Christmas.

Kenny was the center of my life. I'd left my university teaching job to be with him full-time, looking after him by myself while my husband Steve was at work. There was scarcely a moment when Kenny's face wasn't in my sight, his voice within earshot. I carried him with me while I did housework, gave him oxygen from a portable tank when he needed it, took him to all his medical appointments.

One evening in February I drove Kenny home from the doctor's office. The cold wind stung my eyes as I carried him inside. I set him down in the living room to work on his favorite seascape puzzle and went into the kitchen to see Steve. "I was talking to a woman at the doctor's office today whose friend's son had the same condition as Kenny," I told him, trying to keep my voice low. "The boy died when he was just four!"

"No, no, I don't want to die!" Kenny cried, running into the kitchen. I scooped him up in my arms. He gasped for breath.

"Not you, darling, not you," I said, burying my face in his soft blond hair. "I was talking about another boy. Mommy's going to take care of you," I said, as Steve put his arms around us both.

That night, when I tucked Kenny into bed, he looked so small and scared. He blew me a kiss, and then a second one —just like always—and closed his eyes. I sat with him a long time, trying to imprint his features in my mind. His breaths came quick and shallow. *Comfort him, Lord.*

When he woke the next morning, I picked him up and he gave me a big smile. "Mommy, I had a dream about a lady," he said. "She was this big"—he lifted his arm over his head—"and had a long white dress and wings like the one in our picture." Steve and I had a painting of an angel in our room that Kenny loved. "She picked me up to take me on a ride. Then I woke up." He stopped and looked at me, his eyes wide and serious. "But if she really came to take me for a ride, I'd come back 'cause you'd be lonely. I love you, Mommy," he said, reaching his arms around my neck.

"I love you too, my snuggly bear," I said. *Maybe if I just hold onto him*, I thought. *Then no one can take him from me.*

Suddenly, Kenny's body stiffened. He groaned deeply, grinding his teeth, and fell limp in my arms.

"Steve!" I screamed. "Kenny's having an attack!" There was no ambulance service in our rural Missouri town, so Steve grabbed the oxygen tank and we jumped into the car. I administered the oxygen, but Kenny remained pale and unresponsive across my lap. Tossing the mask aside, I bent over to breathe air through my son's dark blue lips. The car jostled as Steve sped down the gravelly road toward the doctor's office. "Don't leave me, Kenny," I whispered between breaths. "Don't leave me."

At the doctor's office, Kenny was taken from my arms and rushed into another room. I sank into a chair, my head in my hands, listening to the doctor and nurses work on my son. At last it was quiet, and I felt Steve touching my shoulder. Slowly I raised my head and met our doctor's eyes. "I'm sorry," he said. "We couldn't save him this time."

We went home to the silence I had dreaded for so long. After a week, Steve went back to work. There was nothing for me to do but ask God how He could take away my son. The emptiness inside me was so vast, I felt I might lose myself in it forever.

"Maybe you could go back to teaching," Steve suggested

gently. But I couldn't deal with the thought of being around strangers. Even Steve and I trudged through our grief separately.

There was no purpose left to my life. I didn't have to get up to make breakfast for Kenny or go to the library for new books to read to him. What use were arms without Kenny to carry? All I could do was think about him.

Week after week, I stared out the window but saw nothing of the passing seasons, only the images that played like a film reel in my mind, from the moment I woke to when I fell into yet another dreamless sleep: Kenny blowing bubbles, licking frosting off a spoon, crawling under the covers with me. And always, always, like a soundtrack, there was his promise: "I'd come back 'cause you'd be lonely. I love you, Mommy."

Then it was the holidays again. The streets stirred with light and color; the heady scent of pine hung in the air. At home, the Christmas boxes remained in the garage. I couldn't bear to see the paper Nativity figures Kenny had cut out the year before for ornaments. *You have taken everything from me, God,* I thought. *How can I celebrate the birth of Your Son when my own son is gone forever?*

On Christmas Eve night I had a dream. I looked up and Kenny was walking toward me holding the hand of an angel. She looked like the one from his dream, with a long white gown and wings. Her hair was the same curly blonde as Kenny's, and her face shone as she smiled at me.

Kenny let go of her hand and ran to me. Ran! He wasn't breathless at all, and his lips were a healthy red. I took him into my arms and settled him on my lap. I stroked his hair, kissed his cheeks, hugged him close. Then he reached up to cup my face in his hands.

"I love you, Mommy," he said. "I told you I would come back."

The angel reappeared. *No, just a little longer*, I thought. *Please*. How could I give him up again? At last, Kenny pulled away. I wanted to go after him, but I could only sit there with my arms outstretched. Kenny ran to the angel and clasped her hand tightly. And all at once I knew I could trust my son to her—that she was taking him to the only One who could care for him better than I. As they walked away, Kenny turned and blew me a kiss—then another— and was gone.

When I awoke, the air felt warm, almost electric. The dream, instead of fading, grew more vivid in my memory. It was like a touch from God, guiding me back to the one thing that could fill the emptiness inside me—His love, the love He'd shown me by giving me Kenny for a few precious years and by letting me visit with him one more time.

I went out into the cool Christmas morning and looked up at the sky, imagining my son's red balloon still floating high among the clouds.

"I love you, Kenny," I said. I knew somewhere, safe in God's embrace, he was blowing me two kisses.

When I Opened My Eyes

by Pat Ciddio

CHRISTMAS IS THE SEASON of surprises. I mean surprise in the deepest sense of the word—the miracle of the unexpected. The kind of miracle that happened to me one Christmas. Not once, but twice.

Christmas Eve, 2001, I was working at my daughter Susanne's jewelry stand at a Denver-area mall. The holidays were her busiest time, so I gave her a hand. It did me good too. With the carols playing over the PA system, the decorations in the store windows and the festive crowds, it was hard to feel lonely at the mall.

Not like at home. The house seemed a rather lonesome little corner of the world this time of year without my husband John. He'd passed away thirteen years earlier, yet there wasn't a day that I didn't think about him. Miss him. I yearned for a connection to him, to his side of the family, even though I knew any hope of that was long gone. John's siblings had died well before him, as had his cousin Ralph from Italy, and we'd completely lost track of their children.

Susanne glanced up from the other side of the stand, where she was rearranging the bracelets, and smiled at me.

I felt my longing give way to gratitude. For the wonderful life John and I had built together, for our children and grandchildren. A person couldn't really expect more blessings than that, could she?

Suddenly a wave of dizziness swept over me. I sat down heavily on the stool by the register. Susanne, still fiddling with the bracelet display, hadn't seen me falter. *Good, since she'd only worry*. My head cleared, and I got to work on polishing some silver charms in a display.

Another wave of dizziness. Worse this time. I gripped the edge of the stand.

Susanne dashed to my side. "Mom, are you okay?"

"I'm fine," I said, brushing her off.

She frowned. "I don't know, Mom," she said. "I'd rather close up early and take you home."

Two women came up, admiring the gold necklaces. "Why don't you take care of those customers?" I said to Susanne. "I'll be all right. This will pass."

I felt better by the time the mall closed. Still, Susanne wasn't taking any chances. She had to go home to her daughter, so she asked her brother Tom to come over and stay the night at my house. "It's nice to have some company," I told him before I turned in, "but, really, you and Susanne are making too much of this."

I awoke to see Tom hovering over me. "Mom, what's wrong?"

"What do you mean?" I sat up. That's when I realized I was on the floor.

"You fell out of bed," Tom said. "That's the second time tonight."

"It is?" How could I have fallen from my bed and have no memory of it whatsoever? Now I was getting scared.

I didn't put up much of a fight when Tom and Susanne insisted on taking me to the emergency room. A doctor examined me and told me it was a case of the flu. I was released with instructions to take it easy.

Almost as soon as I got home, my other daughter, Nancy, phoned from Albuquerque, New Mexico. "Susanne told me what happened." Nancy quizzed me about my symptoms. "I'm going to talk to a friend who's a neuro-surgeon," she said.

Within hours Nancy called again. "Mom, you should never have been released from the hospital. Pack a bag. You're coming here for tests."

"I'll never get a flight," I said. "It's Christmas Day. . . ."

"No, Mom. Just sit tight. I'm coming to Colorado to get you."

Nancy drove 450 miles to pick me up, and turned right around and took me back to Albuquerque, to the hospital where her friend worked. A medical team was waiting. Tests showed my carotid artery, which supplies blood to the brain, was ninety-five percent blocked. That was the reason for my dizziness. I'd suffered a series of ministrokes.

"Pat, you need surgery to clear the artery," Dr. Jacobs said. "But it's risky, and I can't guarantee you'll be one hundred percent afterward. You might not be. That's why it has to be your decision to go ahead with surgery. Not mine and not your kids'."

Scared? Try terrified. But without surgery, I'd almost certainly have another stroke. I couldn't risk that. I wanted more time with my three children and with my grandchildren. What had I been reminding myself Christmas Eve at the mall? That I'd been richly blessed. *Lord, You've always taken care of me*, I prayed. *I'm trusting my life to Your hands —and Dr. Jacobs'—now.*

A prevailing sense of peace settled over me. There was only one place it could have come from.

I woke after surgery, feeling that same sense of peace. One look at my daughter's face and I knew everything had gone well. "Dr. Jacobs put in a stent to keep your carotid open," Nancy said. "He says you'll make a full recovery." We called Susanne and Tom in Colorado to tell them the news. They put my grandkids on to say Merry Christmas. It was like having my whole family gathered in my hospital room around me. I felt a little wistful when Nancy had to leave at the end of visiting hours.

Maybe that's why I was delighted to see a handsome young man poke his head into my room the next morning. "Hello, I'm the hospital chaplain. Is this a good time for a visit?" he asked.

"Of course," I said. "Come in, Chaplain."

He pulled up a chair to my bedside. "I like to greet all the new patients—especially when I share their last name."

"You're a Ciddio?"

"Yes, I am," he said, pointing to his nametag: Walter Ciddio. "I was making a joke. I have never met anyone else named Ciddio."

"Neither have I," I said. "Where are you from?"

"I grew up here in New Mexico. My father was from Italy, though."

It can't be, I thought. Still, I felt compelled to ask, "Your father. Was his name Ralph?"

"Yes! How did you know?"

For a moment I was too moved to speak. "My late husband, John, was Ralph's cousin," I said at last. "That would make me . . ."

"My second cousin," he whispered.

Then he gently put his arms around me and held me close. My second cousin. My sole connection to my husband's side of the family, one I had so yearned for and finally attained.

A holiday that began with a brush with death ended with an incredible reaffirmation—make that two—of life and of the Lord's unceasing love for me. See why I think Christmas is full of surprises? The best kind. Miracles.

Christmas Morning in the Pasture

by Betty Elrod

EMPERATURES DROPPED, but no matter. Our house was warm as toast. I put finishing touches on the holiday decorations. Jackson, our Yorkshire terrier, watched me hang my stocking and then Bill's. He cocked his head.

"Do you think I'd forget you on Christmas Eve?" I pulled out the plaid stocking with Jackson embroidered at the top and hung it next to ours. Jackson wagged his tail. He might not have been able to read his name, but after fifteen years he knew his stocking.

I snaked some garland into the hallway. A pile of Christmas cards lay on the side table by the door. Several of them were addressed to Jackson. "To one of my favorite customers," wrote Jan from the grooming salon. "Merry Christmas!" He also got cards from all of our grandchildren.

Anybody who found it silly for a dog to get this much attention didn't know Jackson. That dog had personality. When I took him for walks, neighbors bent down to talk to him. "You look very handsome in your yellow slicker," a friend told Jackson one rainy day. Jackson ran around in a circle, showing off. Even four-legged neighbors weren't immune to his charms. Our backyard bordered a pasture where horses grazed. They came right up to the wire fence and put their massive heads down low. Jackson wasn't intimidated. He ran over to say hello, barking, jumping, begging to be noticed.

I arranged Jackson's Christmas cards so Bill would see them when he got home from work. Taking care of our little dog was a big focus. But we couldn't protect Jackson from everything. He was getting older. His eyesight was almost gone. He could barely hear. Sometimes he got confused outside and couldn't find his way back to the house. What if something happened when Bill and I weren't home? Who would protect him then?

Jackson barked and hurried into the living room. "You always know the time. Don't you, boy?" I laughed. Right on schedule Jackson climbed up on the couch and watched for Bill. "Somebody got a lot of cards," I sang when he came in, "and it wasn't you or me." Bill chuckled at each one.

We had a quiet evening, just the three of us. After dinner, Bill and Jackson played fetch with a crocheted jingle ball. We turned in early. "Santa won't come till you're fast asleep," I teased Jackson. Bill and I slipped underneath the covers. Jackson curled up at our feet with his stuffed lamb. "Night, Jackson," I said before I drifted off.

I awoke some time later, hearing a bark in the darkness. "Jackson has to go out," I mumbled. I rolled over to look at the clock: 3:00 AM. "Be right back," Bill said. I must have dozed off. This time Bill was shaking me. "What is it?"

"Jackson's gone!"

My eyes darted to Jackson's usual spot on the bed. Only his stuffed lamb was there.

Bill was shivering in his pajamas. "I thought he'd stick close to the porch. I just ran in for my robe."

I pulled on some sweatpants. Bill grabbed a flashlight. We headed for the back door. "Jackson!" I called from the porch. "Jackson!" No answer. An icy wind whipped through my hair. *It's freezing. That old dog won't last out here.*

"Let's ride around," Bill suggested. We went to the car. Bill drove and I searched out the windows. Jackson was nowhere to be found. Bill and I returned home. "Jackson!" we yelled in the yard. I panned a flashlight beam across the bushes. "Here, boy!"

What was that? A faint bark in the distance. Bill and I looked past the fence. "It came from the pasture!" I cried.

Bill helped me over the fence that separated our yard from the field. I hadn't climbed a fence in I don't know how long, but I would have climbed Mount Everest for Jackson. Bill was right behind me. Searching wasn't easy in the dark. The barking—if that's what it was—had stopped. Which way to go? My fingers and toes ached from the cold. "We'll come back in the morning," Bill said finally, sweeping the grass with the flashlight one more time.

Heartbroken, we trudged back to the house. Jackson was cold and alone. No one to protect him. Not even his stuffed lamb for comfort. I wrapped my coat around my shoulders. *Lord, keep Jackson safe and warm*. It seemed like an impossible prayer on a night like this. But anything was possible on Christmas, wasn't it?

It was close to 5:00 AM. Bill and I sat at the kitchen table, waiting for first light. We never said what we both were thinking: We probably wouldn't find Jackson alive. After what seemed like forever, the first rays of dawn appeared through the window. "Merry Christmas," said Bill. "Let's go find our boy."

We headed back to the pasture, empty save for four majestic horses. I'd never noticed how beautiful they were until now. The soft light caught their smooth coats and settled around them like a fleece blanket. "Look, Bill. They know how to protect themselves from this cold." Heads bent toward the ground, the horses stood together in a huddle, warmed by the breaths of one another. It was an almost heavenly scene. Peaceful as it was, though, it only brought tears to my eyes. If those big, strong animals felt the cold, there was no way Jackson could have survived it. My throat was sore from calling. "Maybe we should take the car out again," Bill said.

I called once more. "Jackson!" A high-pitched whine answered. I looked at Bill—he'd heard it too. It came from over where the horses stood. We rushed to them. I squeezed my body into the center of their circle.

"What's going on here?" I asked the gentle creatures.

Something was there on the ground between their feet. A furry animal, curled up tight. I swept aside the tall grass with my hand. A tiny tongue licked my finger. Jackson!

One of the horses tossed its head and snorted proudly. "We took care of him. We kept him safe," the great beast seemed to say. The other horses crowded their large bodies close, blocking Jackson from the wind and warming him with their breath. I gathered our little dog up in my arms and wrapped him in my scarf, rocking him like a baby. Jackson whimpered and licked my nose. "You scared us there, Jackson," Bill said, ruffling his ears.

The horses slowly backed away. They swished their tails and munched the grass, hungry after their night's work. We had quite a story to tell the kids and grandkids over Christmas dinner. Jackson's angels had manes instead of wings!

I didn't worry so much about Jackson after that. I knew in my heart he was watched over. When he died, Bill and I were by his side. I believe angels huddled around us too, comforting our baby like the horses had that peaceful Christmas morning. But this time Jackson's angels had wings.

PART III

Angels of Mercy

He shall give His angels charge over you,
To keep you in all your ways.
They shall bear you up in their hands,
Lest you dash your foot against a stone.

Psalm 91:11–12 NKJV

ABOUT THE TIME CAM BUCKLEY was thinking "maybe there are some wounds that won't ever heal," she met a complete stranger who called her by name and said, "I can see the sadness in your eyes. Don't you know how much God loves you?" There's more to the story, but as a result of that mysterious appearance at the Laundromat, Mrs. Buckley gained strength to deal with the heartbreak of her daughter's death.

Other stories in this section illustrate God's mercy in sending messengers—that's the meaning of the word *angels*—at critical moments: easing the death of a beloved pet, planting a memory that helped ease an impending grief, giving a young woman a reason to "believe in the future"—in faith, with hope.

May these stories assure you that God's messengers of love are at hand, whether or not they make themselves physically known.

Appearance at the Laundromat

by Cam Buckley

W HEN MY TEENAGE DAUGHTER Honey Marie returned to live with my husband Bill and me after spending two years with her father in another state, I looked forward to long, lazy summer afternoons riding horses with her in California's San Gabriel Mountains where we lived. But in an instant those visions went dark. My beautiful daughter committed suicide.

The first few days after it happened, I felt as though I were moving hazily through a nightmare. I had sensed something was not quite right with Honey, but I had attributed it to just another phase. Now it was too late. I couldn't bring myself to go to her funeral, couldn't even go into her room and face her closet filled with crisp, new summer outfits she would never wear. All I wanted was to be alone, far away from anyone who might want an explanation for what I myself could not understand. *Why didn't I know she was so unhappy? Why didn't she come to me? Why, God, did You take my only child?* I sat at my bedroom window for hours, searching for answers.

Bill stayed home from his construction job, taking over the household chores and looking after our horses and pet birds. He tried to coax me out of my isolation, inviting friends over for short visits, making me eat meals with him, or just sitting with me in front of the television. I had always managed to deal with whatever blows life had dealt me, holding my emotions carefully in check. This time I had been knocked to my knees, and I still could not allow myself to express my feelings. Instead, I closed myself off, unable to face a world without Honey.

Late one afternoon Bill sat down beside me at the window. "You've got to get out of the house, Cam," he said gently. "Why don't you go for a walk?"

I shook my head.

"Well then, go riding—just get outdoors. You can't go on like this." I closed my eyes. *I know*, I thought.

I finally pulled on an old T-shirt and jeans and walked out to the stable. My favorite horse, Diablo, nickered in greeting. I saddled him and we slowly rode down the mountain. I was dimly aware of the quails and blue jays fluttering among the pines, the dramatic lines of the cacti, the juniper-covered foothills—all the things I used to love about our land. But what seized my attention now were the shadows, the stumps of dead trees, the lonely howl of a coyote.

A twig brushed my shoulder and I recoiled. A squirrel darted across our path, and I nearly jumped off Diablo.

Everything looked unfamiliar, though I'd traveled that trail countless times. *I have to get away from here!* I turned Diablo around and nudged him into a gallop. At home, I fell into Bill's arms, shaking.

After that episode I didn't venture out alone. Whenever Bill was out of my sight, I was terrified something would happen to him. He turned down one construction assignment after another to stay with me. Every day I resolved to start over somehow, but my phobias paralyzed me. If something as terrible as losing my child could happen, who knew what tragedies might be lurking in the future? I kept thinking the pain would begin to fade, but it didn't. *Maybe there are some wounds that won't ever heal,* I thought.

"Cam," Bill told me one evening two months after Honey's death, "I'm going to go to work tomorrow."

"Please, Bill, you can't leave me alone."

He squeezed my hand. "You're going to be all right. I know we can get through this."

One morning a couple of weeks after he went back to work, I stood in front of our house watching Bill drive away. When his car was out of sight, I went inside to my spot near the bedroom window. I tried to retreat into memories of Honey, but every time our parrots squawked or the house creaked on its foundations, my heart skipped a beat. I became acutely conscious of the sound of my own breathing.

I have to do something or I'll go crazy. I opened my closet to get dressed and saw the hamper overflowing with dirty clothes. The Laundromat was in town, a half hour away. Could I make it? I had to try. I loaded baskets of clothes into my car and started off. The sun shone with a harsh brilliance that made my eyes hurt. I couldn't rid myself of the hollow feeling in my stomach that something was wrong. *What if the car breaks down? What if Bill calls needing help?* Several times I had to stop the car, fearing I was going to be sick. But I kept on.

I reached the Laundromat and peeked inside. Empty. Relieved, I walked through the doorway. As my eyes adjusted from the sunlight, I saw her—a little old lady surrounded by several baskets of clothes. How come I didn't spot her before? She wore an oversize dress and a dark blue sweater that hung to her knees. Her dark face was deeply wrinkled but her eyes were bright. I walked past her to the far end of the row of machines. She smiled and said, "Good morning." I returned the greeting mechanically and hastily began measuring detergent.

While I dropped clothes into the machine, I slowly became aware of her humming, so softly I had to strain to hear it above the swish of the washers. I couldn't quite place the melody. She began making small talk in a low, soothing voice one might use to calm a child. I nodded politely, not really paying attention to what she was saying.

"You know, I've raised many children," she said, her hands moving amid the clothes like tiny birds.

God, please, I don't want to hear this. I concentrated on setting the dials on the washer, yet I couldn't ignore the soft glow in the air. It was all around the room. I rubbed my eyes but it remained.

"Yessiree, many a child has blessed my life," the woman continued. I looked up at her and she moved closer.

"Sometimes you get hurt so badly you think you'll never mend, that no one can make the pain go away." She gave me a luminous smile. "But you do mend, dear. The Lord is right there beside you, even in your darkest moment, even when you think you're all alone."

I was transfixed—by her gaze, by her voice. I seemed to hear nothing else.

"I can see the sadness in your eyes. Why are you punishing yourself so?" She took my hand in hers. "Don't you know, Cam Buckley, how much God loves you?"

Her words broke through my pain like lightning through storm clouds. I didn't will what I said next; it just poured out of me with the tears I had held back so long. I felt I was talking to a lifelong friend who understood me completely. I told her about my daughter, how lost she must have been, how guilty I felt. How I didn't think life could ever be bearable again.

"There now," she murmured when I finished, wiping away my tears with an old handkerchief. "Just you remember how much God loves you. He has a plan for you, as He has for all His children."

She went back to her baskets, again humming that tune I couldn't quite place.

I leaned against the washer, feeling drained yet lighter somehow, as if the grief had finally receded enough to allow room for love and for living again. All because of this stranger. "What is your name?" I asked, turning to face her. I saw no woman, no baskets, no clothes.

"I didn't even know your name," I said. But she knew mine. And then I recognized the tune she'd been humming. It was "Amazing Grace." I used to sing it to Honey when she was a baby. I hummed it quietly while I finished the laundry, and then buried my face in the soft, warm clothes, feeling a comfort I thought I would never find.

Eleven years later, I continue to feel comforted by that mysterious woman's words. When sadness threatens to overwhelm me, I remind myself that God loves me as I love my daughter still. He sent an angel to the Laundromat to show me there is no pain His love can't begin to heal.

Another World beyond Our Own

by Glenda Barbre

OUR NEW HOUSE TILTED SLIGHTLY over the bank above the San Lorenzo River. Eucalyptus trees and acacias grew in a grove behind the back porch, reaching up to the second-floor bedrooms. And in front of the house, the river swept wide and opened into the Pacific Ocean, only about eight hundred yards downstream. We could sit on the front steps and watch the tide swirl and push against the bank.

It was the summer of 1953, and we had just moved from Oregon to California—my mother, father, younger sister and me—and I think all of us hated to leave our mountain cabin for the seashore of Santa Cruz. But even at age twelve, I understood that we had come to find the best treatment for my father's cancer. And though I missed my old friends, I'd have given anything to have my father return to the health he'd had before his illness. He was the solid center of our lives, all his girls flocking around him when he came into the house after his day at work. A woodcrafter by trade, our father had made much of the furniture in our Oregon house. He came home smelling of lumber, his arms sprinkled with sawdust. He would sit at night with his fiddle in his hands, the rest of us singing. Those same hands could snatch a fish right out of the river, a trick he tried to teach me, saying I should ease my hand under the fish's belly and swat it out of the water. "Like a bear," he'd say.

That was Oregon, though. In California, the San Lorenzo ran deep and the banks were too slippery for me to fish from. Still I would go down to the rocks and sit in secret, away from the house where no one could see me by the river. Sometimes I would walk by the river with a friend I'd met, but usually I would sit alone and gaze on the churning water and wish I could turn time back to the mountain and have my father well again.

In the two years that followed our move, it seemed I learned the whole shoreline. And I picked a favorite rock, a big flat smooth one, where I felt safe from the worries of the world. My father went for tests and surgeries, my sister and I taking care of him after we got home from school. He lost weight and needed lots of sleep and shots for his pain. At night, my mother would bring donuts home for him from the shop she worked in to help make ends meet.

Then one afternoon after my sister and I came home from school, my mother and father sat in the living room. "We have to talk to you," my mother said, as my father slowly lifted his eyes to us.

"The cancer isn't going away," he said. "Doctors say I have about a year."

But this can't be happening, I thought. "The doctors in California were supposed to help you!"

"It's out of their hands now," my father said.

I was trembling with anger and fear. "You mean we came all the way here just to have a doctor say that? 'About a year'?"

My father shrugged, his eyes darkening with worry as he lowered his head. "I'm sorry, kid."

I ran to my bedroom and threw my parade baton through the window, the sound of shattering glass bringing my father to my door. "We'd better fix that," he said quietly, bending over to hug me. But I left the house, running toward the river and the comfort of my rock at the water's edge. I gazed over the deep-rumbling river and tide currents, asking God who would fix things once my father was gone.

A few days later, my friend Mary and I were down by the river rocks. "You want to walk up under the train bridge with me?" I asked, shielding my eyes from the sun as we started to pick our way along the lower cliffs of the San Lorenzo. We could see the trestle bridge in the distance upriver—the whole tumbled stretch of rocks empty but for the seagulls soaring on the wind above—and with the last light of the afternoon, Mary and I went climbing and scrambling along the edge. We held tight to the slick logs and rocks, inching along the algae and stones toward the trestle.

"Go slow," I called.

Then I heard the gulls scream and a great splash and turned to the empty shore. "Help!" Mary came up screaming and coughing from the water. I reached to her and leaned as far over the water as I could. The river had moved her away from the shore, and she struggled to grab for my hand. I strained and tried to get hold of her, finally brushing her arm with my fingertips. When she felt my touch, she clutched at my hand in desperation, pulling me off the slick rocks and into the cold waters beside her.

We both panicked and flailed against each other and the water, helplessly fighting the currents that pulled us toward the middle of the river. I fought to keep my head above the water, but Mary tried to climb on top of me. Neither of us could swim, and we clung to each other as the water dragged us down. I couldn't break Mary's hold and couldn't find air, and I knew, in that green darkness, that we were going to die. *God, please help me.*

Then I felt someone grab my hand and pull me through the water. I cut through the river on my stomach, straight for the shore. And that hand, a man's hand, pulled me onto the rocks and placed my fingers into the crevices we had used as footholds. There I lay facedown, coughing and gasping for air.

"Thank you," I sputtered, looking up to the man.

But no one was there. No one was anywhere—not on the bank or on the bridge or the other side of the river.

I knelt on the rocks in disbelief, brushing my hair back and blinking water out of my eyes. No one was in sight, no one but Mary, who lay gasping on the rocks a few feet away. She was trying to say something between coughs. "You saved my life," she said finally.

"I didn't pull you out," I said. "I was drowning, just like you."

We looked at each other and the empty shoreline and didn't say anything all the way home. My mother was in the kitchen and took us into the house and started to get us out of our wet clothes. "What on earth have you two been up to?" she asked. We told her what had happened.

"We're okay, Mom," I said as I slipped off my shirt. "And we'll be okay." I understood now that there lay another world beyond our own, a world much bigger and safer than anyplace I'd ever been, even my rock on the San Lorenzo River.

Through the months leading up to my father's passing, I clung to the hand that had reached down and saved me once already. I held tight to that hand in the last days we had with my father. And I hold that hand still. My rock.

"Something Wonderful Is Going to Happen"

by Sandy Letizia

SOMETIMES, EARLY IN OUR MARRIAGE, for no reason at all, my husband would stop at a flower shop and buy me a dozen roses.

"A whole dozen!" I'd say, overwhelmed and aghast. "Oh, Dave, they're too expensive. We can't afford this."

For a while he didn't hear me. If he saw twelve roses, he'd buy them all. To the Italian romantic, more was better.

But finally, my Scotch-Irish nature got through to him. "Oh, Dave, they're so wonderful—but I just can't appreciate more than one at a time."

Soon he was coming home and handing me a single rose. "For you," he'd say as he planted a kiss on my lips. Eventually, he settled on one rose in particular, an unusual lavender rose that I always gushed over. A sweet, powerful fragrance wafted from its delicate petals.

The longer we were married, the more often he stopped at the florist—for a rose. Or sometimes he bought three, which we both justified by saying that each represented one of our three children.

Ours was a marriage that got better with age—and after being tested by some dark days. In March 1973, Dave, the thirty-seven-year-old athletic director and all-purpose coach at Clear Fork High School, suffered his first major heart attack. When he went back to school in September, he still had a teaching job, but someone had decided to relieve him of his coaching responsibilities.

Over the next twenty-one years, I lost track of how many times I drove him to the emergency room at Mansfield General in Mansfield, Ohio. In addition to numerous heart catheterizations, he had open heart surgery, and eventually they put in a pacemaker. But doctors never really did control the angina attacks, with pain that split through his chest as if it were torn open with a knife.

And for several years right before his doctor prescribed retirement from teaching at age forty-eight, Dave lost control of his emotional pain. Dave's physical stamina had been the core of his identity—as a football player, as a lifeguard honored for saving a child's life, as the eighteen-year-old "hero" who pushed his buddy out of a fiery gas explosion, as an athletic coach. And as that physical stamina slipped, he dulled the pain with drink.

This was not the Dave I knew and loved, but a moody, argumentative, unpredictable stranger. At night I would cry myself to sleep, silently praying, *God, where are You? What's happening to us? Please make it better.*

But, of course, Dave had to make his own decision to "make it better." And with great courage, he admitted himself to a local alcohol treatment center.

He walked out of that hospital a changed man. Just one bit of evidence: That first night home he sat on our bed and said, "Honey, from now on I'd like for us to join hands and pray together at bedtime." Pray together! This would be a new venture, but I was willing, even eager. And that night I prayed, "Lord, thank You for giving Dave back—now better than ever."

Walking with new inner strength, Dave was able to face his early retirement. With time on his hands, he turned his talents toward serving others. He looked after his ailing mother. He was treasurer of the board of a local hospital.

But often his acts of mercy were the random variety. He would drive someone to medical treatments or the airport. We frequently visited a former student who'd been shot and paralyzed on the job as a policeman. He liked to send anonymous cashier's checks to people in hard straits. He was the Good Samaritan type who would stop if he saw a car accident. The first-aid kit in our car trunk was as much for strangers as for ourselves. About the only limit to his generous nature was an agreement we had: We did not pick up hitchhikers. No way. Too dangerous. You never knew who might force you to do what.

There was a second fresh aspect to Dave's retirement years. Always aware of the precarious nature of his health, we valued every minute we had together. When weather permitted, this meant spending the afternoon at Sun Valley pool, open to members and their guests.

We also attended a weekly Bible study, and that's where a friend pointed out Psalm 27:14 KJV: "Wait on the Lord: be of good courage, and he shall strengthen thine heart: wait, I say, on the Lord."

"I felt as if this verse was for you, Dave," she said. Dave and I latched onto the verse, though the two of us saw slightly different meanings in its promise. We both agreed that "strengthen" meant "heal." I was sure God meant to repair Dave's physical heart. Dave, on the other hand, sat me down on the couch one day and said, "Sandy, you know that this heart ailment is someday going to be for keeps. Listen, I want you to remember that when I go to heaven, I'll receive the ultimate healing—no more pain! Please promise me you'll remember that and try to be happy for me."

Don't say it. Don't say it! That afternoon I cried and clung to his chest, wishing he hadn't admitted what I didn't want to hear. No. God was going to heal his heart. Heal his heart. Soon. Very soon.

On September 1, 1993, about noon, Dave and I headed for Sun Valley pool. This day we had broken our usual routine in that we'd taken two cars. When we left the pool about three, I turned left and drove directly home; he turned right, toward Mansfield, intending to drop in briefly at his sister's.

I'd been home for about an hour when Dave pulled his Oldsmobile into the garage. As he walked into the family room, I knew something was wrong. His "Hi, hon" was always followed by a kiss or a hug. But he just stood near the door, no smile, no warmth.

Oh no, not again, his heart, I thought. "What's wrong? Are you in pain?"

"No, that's not it at all," he said as he sat on the couch. "I just had the strangest thing happen. On my way to Margaret's, I saw this hitchhiker. A well-dressed black man."

"You didn't pick him up, did you?"

"Yeah, I did."

"Dave, you know our agreement about picking up strangers. It's just too dangerous."

"I know," he said apologetically. "But twice something told me to pick him up. It was important. I just had to. How often have you seen a black man with blue eyes? This guy had intense blue eyes."

Dave obviously needed to talk and I let him.

"I asked him where he needed to go. He said, 'Just drive for a while, and I'll tell you when to let me off. Normally, I wouldn't be out today, but my boss has a special job for me to do.' After a mile or two of comfortable silence, the guy said, 'You know St. Stephen?' Then I thought I'd picked up some kook.

"I answered, 'No, I don't think so.'

"The guy insisted, 'Oh yes, you do know St. Stephen.'

"I decided this was no one to disagree with, so I played along, 'Well, maybe I do know him.'

"When we got near the corner of Cook Road and Main Street, he said that's where he wanted to get out. I offered to take him farther, but he said no. So I stopped the car, and the guy reached over and squeezed my hand. He looked me straight in the eye. You've never seen such beautiful blue eyes. He said, 'Very soon something wonderful is going to happen to you.'

"That was weird enough, but I know I didn't hear the car door slam when he got out. And when I looked in the rearview mirror and around to the right and left of the car, he wasn't there.

"So what do you make of all that?" he asked, still utterly bemused.

It didn't make any sense at all unless . . . "Dave, I think you've seen an angel."

He looked startled. "Think so?" He thought a minute and said, "I don't know much about St. Stephen. Do you?"

Having attended weekly Bible studies for years, we both felt somewhat biblically literate. But for Stephen, we drew a blank.

"I think I'll call Mary Jo," Dave said. "She'll know." Our neighbor Mary Jo was a devout Catholic. Dave figured she would be familiar with anyone in the "saint" category. I listened again as Dave told Mary Jo his story. I couldn't hear what she said, but suddenly Dave's eyes got real big. He turned toward me and said, "I can't believe it. That's what my wife just said."

I burst out laughing. Mary Jo's analysis confirmed mine; she thought he'd seen an angel.

Mary Jo knew that Stephen was a New Testament martyr, stoned to death. "I'll dig up some more information about him and get back to you," she said.

That night at a meeting, I told three friends the story. Each wondered aloud what "wonderful" future Dave had in store. For two or three days, the angel and his message occupied our thoughts. Dave was pensive, reflective, in outer space, as a kid might say. What wonder might this be?

Then over Labor Day weekend, we went to a picnic at the home of friends we'd known since college days. We were further distracted with earthly matters when Dave had to spend a night in the hospital for observation of chest pain they said wasn't heart related. The hitchhiker faded from the picture, at least in my mind. Mary Jo didn't call with additional information. I didn't look up the Bible story. St. Stephen might as well have never entered our lives.

But on Friday morning, September 10, the racking chest pain once again sent us to the hospital. By one o'clock we were in the emergency room. Doctors and nurses hovered over Dave. He was begging for relief and perspiring like a saturated sponge. His hand clutched at his chest as if he were trying to pull out the pain.

Though the sight was intolerable to me, we'd been here before. I'd repeatedly heard the doctor say the same words: "Sandy, things don't look good. You'd better have your children come."

I called my children, and then for a long time—too long—Dave and I were left alone. I rubbed his back, held his hand. To try to focus my mind on God and not on the horror of Dave grasping at his chest, I pulled from my purse a devotional booklet and started to read.

At one point, after nurses had come back in, David gave a desperate prayer: "God, how many times do I have to go through this?"

I just held on to his hand, until he soon yelled out and lurched onto his side. Immediately, someone grabbed my shoulders and ushered me away from the bed as buzzers went off and the curtains closed.

Dave had come around so many times in the past, I couldn't believe the doctor's five-o'clock words: "Sandy, there was nothing we could do. Dave's gone."

"I want to go too," I blurted. Without him at my side, I didn't want to stick around even one hour.

But I did. I lingered one hour. Two hours. One day. Two days. I greeted more than five hundred people at the funeral parlor, many of them Dave's former students, each sharing a heartening "Mr. Letizia" story.

The day after the funeral, our neighbor Mary Jo came over to visit. Sitting next to me on the living room couch, she listened as I therapeutically rehashed the events of the past week.

I had a long list of what-ifs. "What if the doctors had paid more attention? What if I had pleaded with God to spare Dave's life instead of sitting there reading a devotional? What if we'd gone to the heart specialist in Columbus earlier in the week?"

Mary Jo interrupted and reminded me of her phone conversation with Dave two weeks earlier. "Don't you see?" she said. "The angel was trying to tell Dave that he would soon be going to heaven."

The hitchhiker. An angel. Very soon something wonderful is going to happen.

It took another week for the words to sink in. At our next meeting, my women's Bible study group gathered around my grief. Before we looked at our assigned Scripture, I told them about the hitchhiker, about his message and the mystery of St. Stephen.

As we went around the room, taking turns reading portions of the story of Stephen, God removed the blinders from my eyes. In the first days of the Christian church, Stephen was one of seven men chosen for the particular task of helping the needy, especially the widows. He was the first Christian martyr, and minutes before his death, Stephen turned his face toward the sky and said, "Look . . . I see heaven open and the Son of Man standing at the right hand of God" (Acts 7:56 NIV).

Jesus stood to welcome Servant Dave into heaven just as Jesus had welcomed Servant Stephen. The thought sent goose bumps down my arms. When I connected the hitch-hiker's prophetic words of "something wonderful" with St. Stephen's heavenly vision, my haunting what-ifs washed away with a torrent of tears.

Though only fifty-eight years old, Dave had died in God's good timing.

I tried to hold on to the angel's message and also to Dave's own warning to me, which now was a comfort: "I want you to remember that when I go to heaven, I'll receive the ultimate healing—no more pain! Please prom-ise me you'll remember that and try to be happy for me."

No matter what scriptural or personal assurances you rely on, there's only one way to face the death of a beloved spouse of thirty-six years: one day at a time.

Every morning I awoke and repeated a prayer, begging God for another measure of joy, some small grace that would heal a bit—as the Scottish would say—of my break-ing heart. Some daily grace got me through the autumn and winter. And soon I was well through the spring—and dreading the dawn of June 1, our wedding anniversary.

One morning late in May, my friend Joan called. Did I want to join her and another friend, JoAnne, on a spur-of-the-moment drive to the Kingwood mansion and gardens in Mansfield?

Why not? The sky was sunny, a perfect day; getting out

would be good for me. I'd meet them at the rose gardens, heavy with their first burst of brilliant blossoms.

"Look at this one. And this one!" We'd lean down to smell a red, then a pink or yellow or white variety, each seeming more fragrant and carefully crafted than the last.

Out of the corner of my eye, I suddenly spotted a lavender blossom that drew me away from my friends and down a solitary path. As I savored the velvet petals and the sweet aroma, I retreated into a private world: At home one day when Dave walked in, saying, "Hi, hon, I'm home. Here, I bought you one of your favorite lavender roses. For you!" I wished back the tender moments of my marriage and then glanced at the identifying marker. What was the rose named? Angel Face.

As healing tears again washed over my cheeks, I looked up into the cloudless sky. "O Lord, thank You for this lavish measure of joy. And Dave—thank you, honey, for the roses. All of them—even these."

When I had composed myself, I told my friends about Dave's Angel Face roses.

The garden grief turned to laughter as we walked to our cars. "God and Dave make quite a team," said Joan.

I finished the thought: "Working together to deliver joy. To the widows—like St. Stephen. And through the face of angel roses."

"Be Happy"

by Theodore Kalivoda

*K*AY OFTEN SANG around the house. She loved the music of the big band era, just as I did. I'd been lucky enough to play trumpet with ballroom orchestras when I was young. At home in Athens, Georgia, I sometimes accompanied her on the piano. "Stardust," "Sentimental Journey," wartime songs, love songs—she sang them all. Kay and I were high school sweethearts before our marriage in 1953, and we knew hundreds of what our children called "old" songs. They were fresh as the morning to us. In fact, we loved music even older—hymns from centuries past. Church music seemed as solid as the Bible to me. "Written when God still made miracles," I once commented, always the skeptical college professor. Kay gave me a disapproving look. Her faith was stronger than mine. We both knew it.

One evening in 1988, after teaching classes at the University of Georgia, I opened the front door and heard Kay singing one of her favorite ballads. Before I had the chance to call out to her, she stopped abruptly and burst into sobs. I found her in the dining room and took her in my arms. "Ted," she whispered. "I can't remember the words."

"That's no reason to cry," I said. "I forget little things all the time." When Kay looked at me, I saw fear in her eyes. "I forget big things too," she said.

It started as simply as that, but over the next two years Kay's behavior changed disturbingly. She complained of stiffness and often had trouble walking. Once I came home to see her nursing a bruised arm. "I felt dizzy and fell down," she explained, brushing the incident aside. But she fell again, and I took her to the doctor. "Maybe an inner ear problem," he said, "or hardening of the arteries." Tests were inconclusive. Naturally Kay was upset, and when her problems continued, she became irritable. Not like the Kay I knew at all.

She had regular checkups, and at times, everything seemed normal. Almost. We still attended church every Sunday, but I noticed her hands shaking when she held her hymnbook. I'd play the piano in the evening and Kay would sing, but she sometimes slurred the words. She squinted when she read. "I need new glasses," she said. Her dizzy spells became more frequent. One day she had a car accident when everything blurred out of focus. I immediately took her back to the doctor.

The first diagnosis was Alzheimer's. As Kay's health grew worse, another doctor said Parkinson's. Eventually

Kay was confined to bed, requiring a nurse's care during the day while I was teaching. When I retired in 1991, I was able to be with her all the time. "What's happening to me?" she asked.

"God knows," I said.

Kay squeezed my hand. "You're right," she said, managing a smile.

A specialist was finally able to give us the answer. Kay was diagnosed with progressive supranuclear palsy, a rare degenerative disease affecting the brain. Although I didn't realize it at first, her condition also took its toll on me. Our children came over when they could, but they had jobs and growing families to look after. "Mom needs full-time care," they kept insisting. I was exhausted, but the idea of a nursing home broke my heart, and I resisted it for as long as I could. One afternoon, I finally told my doctor how depleted I felt. "If you don't get help soon," he said, "you won't be well enough to take care of Kay."

The children and I found a good home for Kay in 1997. I visited her every day. She was often disoriented and in pain, fed and medicated through tubes and unable to speak. How I missed the sound of her voice. Remembering her singing around the house, I sometimes played the piano for her and the other patients. The music always seemed to lift Kay's spirits. She communicated with me by squeezing my hand for yes. Once, after I played her favorite hymn, I asked, "Did you like it?" She squeezed with extra effort, and I thought I detected the old sparkle in her eyes.

I prepared for my visits with Kay as I'd once prepared for my classes—finding interesting things to talk about, doing research, making notes. I stayed up late watching television, hoping to discover something new she would enjoy. One night I chanced on a program about angels. I was about to switch channels when I got caught up in a woman's story. She was talking about angels in her life. Not in the Bible, but in her life day to day. An angel had visited her, and she had been healed of her suffering. Kay should be so fortunate, I thought. But I dismissed the idea immediately. Angels in today's world? Never. I was a facts-oriented man, and that was that.

Still, I'd found something interesting for Kay, so sitting beside her the next day, I began telling the story from the TV program. "You won't believe this," I said, when I got to the part about the healing angel. Kay groaned. I thought she was in pain, but when I asked, she moved her head. No, she was saying. "Do you want to hear more about the angel?" I asked. This time, she gave an emphatic squeeze: *yes*.

I continued. Kay groaned again and moved her head from side to side, showing displeasure at my dismissive attitude about the woman's experience. "What do you mean?" I asked. Kay stopped moving, and I saw a hopeful look in her eyes. I held her hand gently. "Are you trying to tell me something?" She squeezed yes. I caught my breath, and then asked, "Do you mean you've seen an angel?" Kay squeezed my hand yes, and she didn't let go.

I sat back in the chair, staring at my dear wife. Never for a moment had I doubted her faith. I didn't doubt her now, but how could she share her experience if she couldn't talk? I stumbled through a series of questions—all the yes-or-no ideas I could possibly think of. Did this happen at home? No. Did this happen in the nursing home? Yes. You saw an angel here? Yes.

Putting together the details of Kay's experience took considerable time. We followed our usual process—a squeeze of my hand when she wanted to reply in the affirmative, her head moving to correct me on the smallest details. I let her eyes tell me when I'd got it just right, just the way she'd tell it.

Here's how her story unfolded: In the middle of the night, when Kay was overwhelmed with pain and sadness, a woman appeared at the foot of her bed. Not a nurse. She was dressed in ordinary street clothes. Kay had no idea who she was or how she could have shown up there. Visitors aren't allowed late at night. The woman remained by her bed for a minute or so, smiling at Kay. She spoke and then left the room.

"What did she say?" I blurted out, forgetting our yes-or-no questions, forgetting that it was impossible for Kay to answer. To my astonishment, Kay opened her mouth, and I heard her speak for the first time in many months.

Her two whispered words astounded me: "Be happy." I let go of Kay's hand and stood up, nearly knocking over my chair. Be happy? What kind of message was that? My wife was dying, and she was supposed to be happy? I was angry, and Kay could see it. With effort she spoke again: "He takes care of me."

I grasped Kay's hand once more, overwhelmed by what she had said. "Be happy. He takes care of me." That was the last time I heard Kay's voice. Soon after, she entered her new life in heaven. Now I believe in the truth of the words she had spoken. The angel meant them for Kay, and Kay meant them for me. God still makes miracles. He sent assurance to a woman of faith and proof to skeptics like me that He is with us today, tomorrow and forever.

PART IV

Reason for Hope

You are my hope, O Lord God.

Psalm 71:5 NKJV

Why are you cast down, O my soul?
And why are you disquieted within me?
Hope in God;
For I shall yet praise Him,
The help of my countenance and my God.

Psalm 42:11 NKJV

OUR CHURCHES OFTEN EMPHASIZE the importance of faith and love. They're great Christian virtues. But how can we thrive without hope?

In Psalm 71, hope is a noun: something we have, something intangible and yet foundationally as solid as God Himself.

But then in Psalm 42, hope is a verb: something we do. "Hope in God" who is "the help of my countenance," the help of my outlook.

Turn the page and you'll find the first of a number of personal stories that combine aspects of the "having" and "doing." You'll see how the God of hope can give His grieving children a reason to hope in the face of loss. In "A Pound of Hope," Janice Asien LaRosa discovers healing through a very earthy vehicle: a furry creature. On the other hand, Norman Vincent Peale engagingly writes of his otherwordly hope: of life after death.

A Pound of Hope

by Janice Asien LaRosa

WHY ARE WE STOPPING at the pet store, Mom?" my daughter Joy asked, her head slumped against the car window. "I thought we were going to Grandma's." Joy's voice was as droopy as her body language. It was, I knew, as hard for her to imagine a world without my mom in it as it was for me. She'd wanted to wear her grandmother's earrings to the funeral and I'd let her. We were going over to my mom's to put the earrings back so everything would be together when we went through my mom's belongings as a family.

"Come in with me," I said. "Snoopy, Elsa and Coco need dog food. Besides, seeing some puppies might make us feel better."

Not that I believed it. Crazy as I was about animals, there wasn't a puppy alive that had a chance of making me feel better. Only Mom's comfort would do that, and she was gone. Joy dragged herself out of the car and came with me into the store.

Two girls chatted behind the counter. "It's so sad about Spooky," one said. "It just breaks your heart, doesn't it?"

"Who's Spooky?" I asked, putting my cans of dog food up on the counter.

"His name's not really Spooky," the other girl chimed in. "We just call him that because he always looks so afraid."

Mom had been afraid at times during her illness. There was nothing I could do to comfort her. "Can I see him?" I asked, the words surprising me. "Just for a second." Joy shot me a look: *What are you up to, Mom?*

One of the girls disappeared into the back. In a flash she was back—with the tiniest dog I'd ever seen. His head lay slack, his eyes closed, and his chest rose and fell as if each breath were going to be his last. The girl gently passed the pup to me. Joy stroked it with her fingers.

The front door jingled and the proprietor walked in. "What is that animal doing out here?" she said to the girls. She turned to me. "I'm sorry, Ma'am. I have other healthy puppies for you to see if you're interested. I don't think this one will last the week."

The woman whisked the dog back where it had come from, and Joy and I paid for the dog food and left. "Mom," Joy said in the car, "wasn't that the saddest little dog you ever saw?"

"It sure was," I said. "I wish there were something we could've done." Just like I wish there had been something I could have done for Mom. But it had been hopeless. We quietly continued on to her house. We went upstairs to put the earrings away.

"It sure feels quiet here without Grandma," Joy said. I opened the jewelry box and put the earrings back. There, tucked away, I spotted an envelope. On the front were two words in Mom's script: "From Janice." I opened it. Inside was a crisp one-hundred-dollar bill. I knew instantly where it had come from. A few years ago I'd found myself with an extra one hundred dollars. Mom was having health problems at the time, so I decided to give it to her to cheer her up. "Do something special with it," I'd told her. "Something that'll make you feel good."

Now, here was that money in my hand again, still waiting to make someone feel good. Mom hadn't spent it. One hundred dollars. Joy read my mind. "Let's go back to the pet store!" she said, a big grin on her face. The first grin I'd seen in days. It was nuts. We had three dogs at home and more heartache than we knew what to do with. But looking at that money, it was almost like Mom was telling me to.

"He's really sick," the pet-store owner said. "I honestly don't know if you two should be doing this."

"We'll see," Joy said confidently. I nodded to the woman. The woman turned to the girls. "Go get the pup," she said. They squealed, as delighted as Joy and I were.

"Spooky just doesn't sound right to me," I said to Joy at home as we cradled our new purchase in a towel warm from the dryer. "Let's call him Franco."

Franco was still wrapped in that towel when my husband Bob came home from work. "What's that?" he asked.

"A puppy," I said.

"Looks more like a mouse," he said, peeling back the towel. "A sick mouse."

"I'm sorry, Bob," I said. "I know it's the last thing we need right now. But Joy and I couldn't resist." I was waiting for Bob to ask how much he cost when the phone rang. It was the lady from the pet store.

"I've been thinking about Spooky," she said. "Thank you for buying him, for giving him a chance. I'm having my vet give you a year of medical treatment—for free."

The next morning Joy and I brought Franco to the vet. "The X-rays show one collapsed lung and pneumonia in the other," he said. "I'll give you some medicine, but there's not much hope." Franco had yet to lift his head or even stand. He wouldn't even eat baby food from my finger. His eyes stayed shut most of the time. But when they were open, I saw a flicker of hope in them. Of determination. I wasn't going to let that flicker go. I took Franco to the vet every few days. None of the antibiotics seemed to do much good, but the glucose shots kept him from fading away.

After ten days the vet told me what I'd been fearing. "I'm sorry. There's nothing else I can do for him. He's just not rallying. He won't eat and that's a bad sign. You did what you could, but I think you should take him home and make him as comfortable as you can. He's probably not going to make it through another night."

I walked out of the vet's, got into my car and started to

cry. All the loss, all the pain of Mom's passing seemed to flood in on me as I stared down at that hopelessly small, hopelessly sick creature curled in my lap. I did as the doctor suggested. I took Franco's favorite washrag, warmed it in the dryer, wrapped him in it and curled up on the couch with him.

"What did the vet say, Mom?" Joy asked when she got home from school.

"Franco's not doing too good," I said. "But we're not giving up on him." I wasn't going to stop believing in that little dog, no matter what. *Lord*, I said, *if I give up on Franco, I'm giving up on hope. Please, You've got to do something....* The rest of my prayer was lost in my tears. God had been good to me through so many struggles in my life. I had to believe He'd stay with me now. I felt Franco's breathing against my chest, each breath a pulse of hope. I picked up a jar of baby food, opened it, dipped my finger in and held it under Franco's tiny black nose. He raised his head, sniffed at it. Then, for the first time ever, his tongue peeked out.

"Franco!" I gasped. "You're eating!"

I slept with Franco on the couch that night. The next morning he ate some more. That afternoon he took a few steps toward Joy, and—another first—wagged his tail. From then on, each day brought a few more steps. Joy came with me on our next visit to the vet. The vet shook his head in disbelief. "He's tipping the scale at a pound! I think this dog's going to make it."

Yes, he was. And so was I. The pain of Mom's passing would never go away completely. But I knew a measure of comfort. That had been the will of God, a God who loves all His creatures, a God of hope. Mom's final gift to me—the little dog in my arms—had been a testament to that.

Bonnie

by Betty R. Graham

I WAS AS NERVOUS AS A CAT as I walked into the gray
stone building to begin my new summer teaching position.
Lord, help me to learn, I silently prayed, as my supervisor
introduced me to the children I'd be teaching. I felt so
inadequate, with only one year's teaching experience, none
of which was with severely handicapped students. I was
young, newly married, and anxious to prove that I could
handle any challenge. Besides, we needed the money for
rent and food while my husband continued his studies in
college.

But on that first day, I didn't feel very brave as I looked
at the six children I'd be teaching, only one who could
speak aloud and all sitting in their wheelchairs specially
designed to each child's individual infirmity caused by
cerebral palsy.

It only took one day to learn that each child could com-
municate even without speech. It was up to me to learn
how. Some who had the use of their arms could point to
the words yes or no painted on the trays attached to their
chairs. Others could only look at those words to answer. As

long as I phrased my questions in a form that could be answered with a yes or a no, we could carry on a conversation easily.

There was one child, eight-year-old Bonnie, who could not control any part of her body except her eyes, so she communicated by looking up to say yes, and down to say no. I soon learned that she was the most intelligent child I had ever taught. Her arms and legs were strapped to her chair to keep her from hurting herself when her arms flailed out involuntarily. She seemed content with this arrangement.

The children lived at the institute year-round, but every three months classes stopped and the children could go home to their families for two weeks. Some whose families lived in other states or countries were able to go home only once a year, and a few never left the institute. But Bonnie's family took her home every chance they got. She looked forward to the trip each time. They lived close enough to visit her on weekends too. She was a happy child.

Once a week we wrote letters home to the parents. I'd sit with each child and write what he or she wanted to say. It wasn't hard because they all wanted to share most of the same news with just a few individual comments for each child. From time to time some parents would answer the letters, which was always cause for celebration for a child. But Bonnie's mother wrote almost every day. I remember thinking how much this mother loved her child. And

I realized how much I loved my new job and decided not to quit at the end of the summer but continue at the institute.

Then the Christmas vacation came, and my husband and I went home to visit our own families. I looked forward to returning to my students two weeks later. But when I walked in the building, my supervisor called me to her office.

"We have some sad news," she said. "While Bonnie was home, her mother had a heart attack and died. Her father, overcome with grief, brought Bonnie back here immediately. He said not to tell her about her mother—that she would forget about her soon."

"Oh, how terrible for that poor girl," I said. "And for her father, too, but his grief has him all confused. It happened so suddenly."

"I know," my supervisor said. "But we must obey his wishes."

With a heavy heart, I went to my classroom. Most of the children seemed happy and eager to share their news of the Christmas holiday. But when the attendant wheeled Bonnie into the room, I was appalled. Her normally happy face was pale with worry. She thrashed in her chair constantly, rubbing her back against the chair. Her usual smile was gone, and her dark eyes seemed set deeper in her face. She'd lost weight and was obviously in anguish. Her eyes pleaded for answers, their normal brightness veiled by tears. My heart broke just looking at her, knowing the cause of her worry and not being able to help her. All I could do was avoid those eyes and talk to the other children about happy times.

This went on for weeks, and Bonnie seemed to waste away in front of me. Her constant thrashing in her chair caused a huge boil-like sore on her back. Every weekend her father and brother came to visit her, as they had before, but they still told her nothing about her mother. The daily letters stopped coming, and my hardest time was spent when I wrote Bonnie's letter home. I knew what she wanted to say, but I had to avoid that subject. Every night when I went home, I prayed for guidance to let me find a way to help her.

After a month passed with no change, my prayers got stronger. *Why, Lord,* I'd ask, *does this small child have to suffer? Can't I do something to help her? Please show me the way.*

That Sunday night when I went to sleep, I dreamed. A woman was standing at the foot of my bed, someone I didn't recognize. But almost instantly I knew it was Bonnie's mother. I had never met either of Bonnie's parents. They came on weekends, and I didn't work on weekends. The woman didn't speak; she just smiled at me. I could feel love in that smile, and I knew how much she had loved her daughter, the child I loved as well.

When I awoke, I made a decision. Bonnie will get her

answers, I vowed to myself. I sat down and wrote a letter to Bonnie's father, asking him to explain to his daughter what had happened. I told him that he might not realize how intelligent Bonnie was and that she would be able to accept what had happened and know that it wasn't anything she had done to cause the tragedy. I poured my heart out to him in that letter and almost begged him to talk to Bonnie when he came to visit on Saturday. Then I put a stamp on the letter and mailed it. I realized that I could possibly lose my job for taking that action, but for some reason, it didn't worry me much. I just prayed that God would help Bonnie.

When I went in to work the next morning, I felt stronger. Without saying a word to my supervisor, I began a discussion of death. I asked the children if they had ever had a pet that had died. Several of them signed their answers, and Elizabeth, the one girl who could speak, told of losing her favorite cat some years ago. I asked if she knew where the cat went after it died. Bless her! She said, "To heaven." When I asked if anyone knew what heaven was like, Elizabeth began to describe the most beautiful place in her imagination, where no one hurts anymore and everybody is happy. Some of the children nodded in agreement. I couldn't think of any words to add to her description.

All this time, I was careful not to look at Bonnie. I was afraid that I'd break down in front of her. But I knew she was listening and thinking. All week we continued our discussion about heaven, the children showing great interest. But I continued to avoid Bonnie's eyes, although she seemed a little calmer that week.

On Friday, I made another decision. I spoke to Bonnie privately.

"Bonnie," I began. "You're worried, aren't you?" Her eyes went up in agreement. "You're worried about your mother, aren't you?" This time her eyes shot up so hard that her whole head rocked. "Well," I said, "you will get your answers, I promise you. Your father is coming this weekend to see you, and I think he will explain a lot of things you have wondered about." I saw the beginning of a smile cross her lips. "But if he doesn't tell you what you want to know," I continued, "I promise that I will when I come to work on Monday."

It was a pretty rash decision. I risked losing the job I liked more than any other job I'd ever had, but somehow inside, I felt it was the best way.

That was the longest weekend of my life. I wondered if Bonnie's father had come and if he had read my letter and decided to listen to me, an inexperienced young woman he didn't know, or if he had been angry and would see that I was punished, and then I'd have to keep my promise to Bonnie. And yet, there was a calmness inside of me. I didn't regret what I'd done.

On Monday morning, when I went to work, my supervisor called me in her office again. *Here I go*, I thought. *I guess I'm out of a job.* But my supervisor told me that Bonnie's father had talked to her. She said that Bonnie cried for a few minutes and then seemed to breathe a sigh of relief. That terrible burden was lifted off her shoulders. My shoulders felt lighter too. I still had a job.

When I walked in my classroom, Bonnie was already in her place. The color was beginning to return to her face, and a slight smile crossed her lips. We talked for a few minutes about her mother and that she was in heaven. Bonnie seemed to be happy about that.

From that time on, we could talk about Bonnie's mother in class. Bonnie seemed to enjoy talking about her. She continued to do her school work as she had before the Christmas break. I, too, felt a closeness with her mother, as if I had really known her when she lived.

Hope and Heaven

by Sharon Betters

*I*N JULY 1993, A TRAGIC ACCIDENT in Delaware took the life of sixteen-year-old Mark Betters, youngest son of a parsonage family. Here Mark's mother relays part of the family's journey through grief, toward hope.

⁊⁊

There is danger in longing to know about things that God doesn't explain, and there is a tendency in our world to proclaim as truth those things that are not. We tested every glimmer of heaven by the grid of God's Word. We placed no hope in anything that was not His truth. But our emotional and spiritual senses were on full alert as we slogged through the pathway of grief. Young Chuck had a particularly interesting conversation with a stranger that puzzles us to this day.

Early in 1993, before Mark died, our son Chuck first heard and then saw a stranger in the church building before services on a Sunday morning. He heard a man wailing. Following the sound, he found a middle-aged balding man prostrated on a classroom floor. He was crying out in prayer, not for himself but for our community, for the children of the world, for the wayward teenagers, for people to repent. Chuck left him alone and went back to the sanctuary to practice his piano playing. But soon the man came and talked to him.

Chuck explains, "I had never met a man like this before. His face was red and swollen from crying, yet he was a burly fellow—a man's man—not someone you would mess with. He had a maturity about him, not unstable as you might infer from his great display of emotion."

He said he was a truck driver who just happened to stop at the church to pray. They talked about the church and about his burden for people to turn to Jesus. He left before the service.

But after that, every month or so, he showed up again, crying out in prayer in a classroom. If Chuck was in the building, the trucker would talk with him, offer encouragement or prayer and then leave. Chuck says, "I remember thinking that this guy was different—nothing bad—just something different."

Then Mark was killed in July. And in September young Chuck began having vivid dreams, even visions, of Mark playing drums. He says,

I would wake up in the middle of the night and "see" Mark playing the drums in my room. I can still see the angle of him playing—his body and the drums were outlined in white—a surreal vision. The first couple of times, I wrote it off as hallucinations. The third, fourth and tenth times I knew it was real. . . . This continued—not every night, just now and then. Then one night I also heard music, a song, even a genre, unlike any I have ever heard before. I believe I was hearing heavenly worship. I was wide awake watching and hearing this in my room at home. I grew scared as the music faded, and I began to cry, because I missed Mark. The reality of the situation was I wouldn't really be with and see my brother for fifty to sixty years if I lived a normal life. My brother wouldn't be at my wedding, be Uncle Mark to my kids, play on our softball teams, play drums on our worship team. . . . That was the reality of things. And it made me very sad. . . .

I know that many people who are wiser and smarter than I might roll their eyes at my story. . . . But nothing I saw is against God's Word. Mark is in heaven. He is worshiping God. It's easy for me to believe that God has perfected Mark's musical skills and that he is one of the great cloud of witnesses who are worshiping in heaven.

The next morning Chuck went to the church. And guess who was there? The praying, crying truck driver. Chuck explains,

> He hadn't been by for a while. I really didn't feel like talking to him. I thought I'd slip into the church

office and avoid him. Sure enough he found me. I said, "hi" and then turned to some task, trying to make it obvious that today wasn't a good time to shoot the breeze. He talked to our secretaries, but after a while I could feel his gaze on me—almost looking through me. I turned toward him and saw his eyes; they looked like blue lightning. When he spoke to me, the room froze. The other people in the room didn't hear him speak; only I did. "Do you know what heaven's like, Chuck? I'll tell you about heaven because I've seen it. There are great reunions of loved ones every day. It is real—don't worry about anything—it's real, and you'll see your brother again."

That was the last time Chuck saw the truck driver, which he—and we—believe was no ordinary trucker but an angel (Hebrews 13:2) sent to remind us of the heavenly home that awaits us.

Chuck says, "God promises to raise my dead body when Jesus comes back. Why would I think it's too hard for Him to send an angel disguised as a truck driver to turn my heart toward the truth? I think He condescends sometimes to meet us right where we are, never at the expense of His Word and never by adding to His Word (Joel 2:28). Our family needed revival. We needed God to pour His Spirit all over us. This was one of those moments where He gave me hope that He was doing just that, in His way, His time."

I Believe in Life after Death

by Norman Vincent Peale

M y FATHER, WHO DIED at eighty-five after a distinguished career as both a physician and a minister, struggled
against a very real fear of death. But not long after he died,
my stepmother dreamed that he came to her and told her
that his fears had been groundless.

"Don't ever worry about dying," he said to her. "There's
nothing to it!" The dream was so vivid that she woke up,
astounded. And I believe that my father did come to reassure her because that is precisely the phrase I had heard
him use a thousand times to dismiss something as unim-
portant or trivial.

In 1939, when news reached me that my mother had
died unexpectedly in another town, I was alone in my office,
numb with grief and loss. There was a Bible on my desk, and
I put my hand on it, staring blindly out of the window. As I
did so, I felt a pair of hands touch my head, gently, lovingly,
unmistakably. The pressure lasted only an instant; then it
was gone. An illusion? A hallucination caused by grief? I
don't think so. I think my mother was permitted to reach
across the gulf of death to touch and reassure me.

And when I was preaching at a Methodist gathering in Georgia, I had the most startling experience of all. At the end of the final session, the presiding bishop asked all the ministers in the audience to come forward, form a choir and sing an old, familiar hymn.

I was sitting on the speakers' platform, watching them come down the aisles. And suddenly, among them, I saw my father. I saw him as plainly as I ever saw him when he was alive. He seemed about forty, vital and handsome. He was singing with the others. When he smiled at me and put up his hand in an old familiar gesture, for several unforgettable seconds it was as if my father and I were alone in that big auditorium. Then he was gone, but in my heart the certainty of his presence was indisputable. He was there, and I know that someday, somewhere, I'll meet him again.

We don't try to prove immortality so that we can believe in it; we try to prove it because we cannot help believing in it. Instinct whispers to us that death is not the end; reason supports it; psychic phenomena uphold it. Even science, in its own way, now insists that the universe is more spiritual than material. Einstein's great equation indicates that matter and energy are interchangeable. Where does that leave us, if not in an immaterial universe? The great psychologist William James said, "Apparently there is one great universal mind, and since man enters into this universal mind, he is a fragment of it."

This intangible in all of us, this fragment of the universal mind, is what religion calls the soul, and it is indestructible because—as James said—it is at one with God. The Founder of Christianity said specifically that there is a life beyond the grave. Not only that, Jesus also proved it by rising from the dead Himself. If you believe it happened, death should hold little terror for you. If you don't believe it, you are really not a completely fulfilled Christian.

The Easter message is one of such hope and joy that even unbelievers are thrilled by it. Last year a reporter I know covered the sunrise service that is held each Easter on the rim of the Grand Canyon. It was cold—below freezing, actually—and he had not worn an overcoat. Not a particularly religious man, he stood there shivering dolefully and wishing himself back in bed.

"But then," he told me, "when the sun cleared the canyon rim and light poured into that stupendous chasm, I forgot all about being cold. One moment everything was gray, formless. Then came torrents of light plunging down the canyon walls, making them blaze with color, dissolving the blackness into purple shadows that eddied like smoke. Standing there, I had a most indescribable feeling, a conviction that the darkness that had filled the great gorge was an illusion, that only the light was real, and that we silent watchers on the canyon rim were somehow a part of the light. . . ."

Strange words, coming from a hard-boiled reporter, but close to a profound truth. Darkness is powerless before the onslaught of light. And so it is with death. We have allowed ourselves to think of it as a dark door, when actually it is a rainbow bridge spanning the gulf between two worlds. That is the Easter message.

Yet there are people, even good Christians, who accept it with their minds but really never feel it in their hearts. I know this from personal experience—the message never got through fully to me until I went to the Holy Land and saw with my own eyes the hills and fields and roads where Jesus actually walked.

One day we visited the beautiful little village of Bethany. This was the home of Mary and Martha and Lazarus. And there is still a tomb there, said to be the tomb of Lazarus. We went into the tomb, down twenty-two steps and saw the place where the body of Lazarus is presumed to have lain until the voice of Jesus wakened him from the dead. I was so deeply moved that, when we came up out of the tomb, I turned to my wife and said, "We are standing where the greatest statement ever uttered was made: 'I am the resurrection, and the life: he that believeth in me, though he were dead, yet shall he live'" (John 11:25 KJV).

At that moment, for the first time in my life, Easter really happened to me, and I shall never be the same again.

In Justin's Room

by *Allison West*

*O*NCE A MONTH I gather with some friends in my son Justin's bedroom to sort and package bags of toys. Several people fold quilts while others cut up sheets of construction paper to make get-well cards. Beanie Babies, crayons, coloring books and Lego pieces are strewn all over the carpet, just as they were when Justin was there—before he lost his battle with cancer.

The word *cancer* is horrifying enough to parents of a six-year-old who are sitting in a hospital, waiting to find out once and for all why their son has been sick for so long— vomiting, sudden breathing lapses, backaches, night terrors —but imagine hearing these words: pediatric neuroblastoma, stage four.

"It's the most advanced stage," the doctor explained. "This type of cancer is usually fatal—partly because it's so hard to diagnose. Unfortunately your son's cancer has already spread to his bones."

Just ten percent was what we learned Justin's chances were. But that was enough for my husband, Lonnie, and me to cling to as Justin began a regimen of aggressive chemotherapy and radiation. Ten percent to us was as good as one hundred percent. Justin had to get better. I could not imagine the world without him. He was my baby, and he was simply the joy of my life. Everything was an adventure to Justin, whether he was putting together his latest Lego set with his nine-year-old brother Cory or adding a new card to his fabulous Pokémon collection. He had a way of filtering out the bad stuff in life and focusing on the good.

In fact, in those first tough weeks after the diagnosis, I think it was more him comforting me than vice versa. "Don't worry, Mommy," he said, wrapping his thin little arms around my neck after one chemo treatment. "I'm feeling better. I'm going to draw a picture of you with the cool markers the nurse gave me."

Each time he went into the hospital, I made goodie bags stuffed with puzzles, toy cars and his favorites—Lego blocks and Pokémon cards—to help him pass the time. A Beanie Baby dog named Bernie was his constant companion through the progressively longer hospital stays. A particularly difficult treatment called for something special: a cardboard box painted as a pirate's treasure chest filled with shiny beads that brought a sparkle back to his eyes. But there was another reason for making the bags: They kept me busy too—so I wouldn't have to think too much about the future, about the unthinkable. Sometimes watching Justin sleep, I'd be overcome by panic. "Please don't leave me, Justin," I whispered. "I won't know what to do without you."

Justin stayed upbeat even as his strength waned. Sometimes all he could manage was sitting by the window with a book. Or watching Cory play video games. He sought comfort in the smallest of things—like a windup toy or a comic book from the latest goodie bag.

Then came what I thought was the miracle I'd prayed for: Justin had a stem cell transplant and soon went into remission. The storm inside me quieted. I cherished every moment with my son. I longed for him to get back from school each day. I didn't even care how messy his room got; Justin was home!

Nine months into Justin's remission, we took him in for a regular checkup. Afterward we were called into the doctor's office while Justin played in the waiting room. One look at the doctor's face and I knew the cancer was back. I didn't say anything, but Justin saw my expression on the way home and asked, "What's wrong, Mom?"

I took a deep breath. "The tests showed your cancer is back."

Justin pursed his lips. He was quiet. Then he said, "Is that why the nurse gave me five Pokémon cards today?"

I couldn't bring myself to answer.

"Okay, so the cancer's back," he said. "But I got five Pokémon cards, and I didn't have to stay over in the hospital. It's still a great day."

Justin started another unforgiving schedule of chemo and radiation treatments. And I was back to putting together goodie bags. During one stretch in the hospital, Justin was moved into a room with another cancer patient, a little boy of four. I only saw his mom visit. We'd been so lucky. Lonnie's coworkers had pooled their accrued sick leave and given it to him so he could be with Justin. And I had a list of more than one hundred people who'd offered to do whatever they could to help us. I e-mailed regularly to update them on Justin's progress.

One afternoon I sat playing cards with Justin. The boy in the next bed stared blankly at the television, clutching a worn teddy bear. I looked back at my son, shuffling the cards. He was surrounded by toys from the latest goodie bag. "Justin," I said, "would it be all right if I gave some of your toys to that boy?"

Justin gave the other boy a long look. Then he dug into the bag and pulled out some things. "Do you think he'd like these?" he asked, handing me a Lego set and a couple of Pokémon cards. I nodded and gave them to the boy. His face lit up like a sunrise and he stammered a thank-you. I too felt a little lighter somehow, as if giving that boy happiness had taken away some of the pain of Justin's illness. *This is how Justin does it*, I thought. *He finds some way to make the best of every situation.*

That became tougher as his condition worsened. His last hope was a stem cell transplant from Cory. The procedure was a success, but Justin soon contracted acute respiratory distress syndrome, a severe breathing disorder that ravaged his lungs. He lapsed into a coma. "He's not going to wake up," the doctor told us. "You need to decide how long to continue life support."

That wasn't a question I allowed myself to ask. We couldn't stop fighting now, not after everything Justin and our family had gone through.

Every day for five months I sat by his pale, still body and held onto his hand as tight as I could, determined to keep him in this world, though the doctors said it was hopeless. The mothers of his schoolmates had brought a quilt made of silk-screened pictures of Justin and our family. I hung it up over his bed so he'd be surrounded by love. I prayed, *Don't take him from me, God.*

One afternoon I'd just whispered those words and opened my eyes. There was my son hooked up to the huge machines, his skin almost translucent. For a moment I couldn't remember his eyes. That's when it hit me: My son was already gone. The smiling little boy with his Pokémon cards and Lego sets was lost somewhere in this wasted body. I laid my hand on his forehead, brushed his cheek with my lips. "It's okay, baby," I said. "If you need to go, it's okay." I bent over and laid my head beside him to look at him, trying to memorize every detail of his face. *I don't want him to suffer anymore. I give him back to You, Lord. Take him into the light.*

We took Justin off life support on Monday, December 11, 2000, and as I said good-bye to my son, I felt like God was gently taking Justin's hand from mine. I leaned on my husband's arm, our footsteps echoing down the hospital corridor. We drove home through the streets, the houses lit up with Christmas lights, and I pictured my son running among a thousand times as many lights and not having to catch his breath.

But that didn't make it any easier to wake up the next morning and realize there was no need to go to the hospital. No need to buy toys for the goodie bags. No more desperate prayers for my son's life. It was over.

I tried to stay positive as I knew Justin would have wanted. Cory had a school Christmas program and I made myself go. *This is how I'll get through it. I'll just do what I need to and not think about anything.* We buried Justin in the quilt the mothers made, with his Beanie Baby Bernie and his favorite Pokémon cards.

Teachers who'd known Justin for just one semester came to say good-bye to my son. Strangers who'd heard about him through church wrote to offer their condolences. Yet I drew away from the people who rallied around me. I was haunted by an emptiness that wouldn't be filled no matter how many household chores I did, no matter how many times I tucked Cory in at night.

One morning I woke up and sleepily headed down the hall to wake up Justin before I realized what I was doing. I sank down on his bed. It was so unbearably quiet in the room, everything suspended as though in a still life. A half-finished Lego set sat in a corner, Pokémon cards were fanned out on the desk, a crayon drawing hung on the wall. Justin had taken such joy in these simple things. They had kept him going. How could I keep going? *He was my world, God. You know that. What is there left for me to do now?*

I spotted a couple of goodie bags I'd made for Justin that I'd never had a chance to give him. I thought of the boy in the hospital to whom we'd given some of Justin's toys. How many other children were still suffering as my son had?

I filled up a few bags with toys and drove to the hospital as I'd done so many times with Justin. I handed the bags over to one of the nurses who used to care for my son. "Please give these to whomever you think needs them most," I told her.

At home I filled more bags with toys. Then I thought of all the people who had supported and encouraged us through Justin's illness. Maybe helping us had made them feel the way I felt giving away the goodie bags. Maybe they would want to help others too. I sent an e-mail to every one of them.

And that's why now a group of us gathers in Justin's room once a month to put together goodie bags for all those kids still struggling with illness like my son did for so long. We sew quilts like the one the moms made for Justin.

We stuff bags with Beanie Babies and magic markers and books. Sometimes I can almost feel Justin there with us, running from one person to another to help, his smile lighting up the room.

There's now a reason to get up in the morning. There's a reason to go out and shop for little presents. And most of all there's a reason to pray again—for all the kids we make the goodie bags for, inspired by Justin's optimism and warmth. So you see, after all the presents I gave to him, the best gift of all turned out to be from my son to me.

PART V

Glimpses of Good-Bye

You hold me by my right hand.
You will guide me with Your counsel,
And afterward receive me to glory.

Psalm 73:23–24 NKJV

"HOW WILL I FIND HEAVEN? I don't know where it is."
Startled by her son's question, Katherine Krahling thought
quick enough to reply: "When the time comes, you won't
have any trouble." Her assurance that he would not be alone,
that God would show him the way, is portrayed in the other
personal stories in this section: mourners who were allowed
a spiritual glimpse of a loved one's leave-taking, a spirit's
departing moment, a heavenly homecoming . . . a glimpse
that made the physical loss a little more bearable. As
Natalie Kalmus says, "I had seen for myself how thin was
the curtain between life and death. . . . Never again will
death frighten me." She was certain of being welcomed
into glory.

A Glimpse of Heaven's Glory

by Janet Franck

I DON'T KNOW WHY tragedy struck our family that bright October morning. Nor why I, of all people, should have been allowed that glimpse of glory. I only know that a presence greater than human was part of the experience from the beginning.

The strangeness started the evening before, when I allowed six-year-old Travis to play outside past his bedtime. I'd never done this before. Travis' two younger brothers were already asleep in bed, and he should have been too; he had to go to school in the morning, after all. But Tara, the little girl who lived across the street, was playing outdoors late too. Though Tara was a year older, there seemed to be a special bond between her and Travis. I heard their happy shouts as they played hide-and-seek under the enormous stars—just as I used to, here in our little mountain town of Challis, Idaho.

And then, later, when I'd called him in at last and he was in his pajamas, he'd suddenly grown so serious. . . .

"Mommy?" Travis had finished his prayers as I sat on the edge of his bed. He took his hands and placed them tenderly on my cheeks. Such a solemn little face beneath the freckles!

"What, Babe?" I smiled.

"I . . . just love you, Mommy," he said, searching my eyes. "I just want you to know that I love you."

The words remained with me as I got ready for bed. Not that it was unusual for Travis to show affection. His outgoing nature had become even more so after he accepted Jesus as his Savior at age five. Little children who know Jesus seem to bubble over with love for the whole world. It was the intensity—almost the urgency—with which he'd said the words that was unlike him.

As I lay in bed that night, the sense that something out of the ordinary was about to happen stayed with me. Our house is small; since my mother came to stay with us, I've shared a bedroom with the children. I could hear their soft, restful breaths as they slept. That wasn't what kept me awake. Nor was it the empty space beside me—my husband was now married to another. Yes, our family had certainly had its moments of pain, but our faith had brought us this far.

I thought back to that time, four years before, when I'd realized my need for the Savior and invited Him to take over my struggle. How magnificently He had! So much help had been lavished on us going through the divorce, the changed lifestyle, the financial difficulties. From our pastor and church friends, I'd gained strength and hope.

But it was the conversion of little freckle-faced Travis that brought me the day-by-day lessons.

"Why are you worried, Mommy?" Travis had said so many times, a hint of impatience in his wide brown eyes. "You have Jesus. We'll get the money for that bill." And we always did.

Two AM. "I love you, Mommy" still pealed in my ears like some distant, gentle bell. I remembered that as my closeness to Jesus increased, my spirit would sometimes hear messages from Him.

I am preparing Travis for something, I'd heard this silent voice tell me, many times. And this did seem to be the case. Hadn't there been that night a couple of months ago. . . ? I'd awakened before daylight and noticed Travis sitting on his bed . . . just sitting, in the purple predawn.

"What's the matter, Babe?" I had asked him.

"Don't you see them?" He sounded disappointed.

"See what?"

"These two angels."

I breathed in sharply; I saw only the familiar room. The boy was wide awake, perfectly calm. I asked him if he was afraid.

"No, Mommy," he'd said. I waited by his bed a little while. Then he said, "Okay, they're gone, you can go to bed now." That was all. But thinking back on that experience, I felt again that sense of the extraordinary pressing close upon us.

The morning of October 28 dawned bright and still. There was the usual bustle of getting breakfast, finding socks that matched, pencils with erasers and so on. Ten minutes before the time he usually left to walk to school, Travis became suddenly agitated: "Mommy, I've got to go now."

"Babe, it's early. You've got lots of time. Sit down."

"I've got to go now! I've just got to!" Travis cried.

"Why?" I asked in bewilderment. He mumbled something about his teacher, about not being late. It didn't make sense; he was never late. "Wait a few minutes," I insisted. "Finish your cocoa."

"Mommy, please!" To my amazement, big tears were rolling down his cheeks.

"All right, all right, go ahead," I told him, shaking my head at the commotion. He dashed out the door, a hurrying little figure pulling on a tan jacket. Across the street, little Tara was coming down her walk. I saw the two children meet and set off toward Main Street together.

Five minutes later I was clearing away the breakfast dishes when it happened. A shudder of the floor beneath me; then a hideous screech of writhing wood. There had never been an earthquake in Challis, but I knew we were having an earthquake now. I ran from the house calling over my shoulder, "I've got to get to Travis!"

I was at the driveway when another tremor flung me against the car. I waited till the earth stopped heaving and then climbed into the driver's seat.

I'd gone two blocks when I saw a woman standing beside a pile of rubble on the sidewalk, the debris of a collapsed storefront. The look on her face was one of nightmare horror. Unrolling the window, I was surprised at the calmness of my voice as I asked, "Was someone . . . caught?"

"Two children," the white face said thinly. "One in a tan jacket. . . ."

I drove swiftly on. Past people running toward the damaged building. Around the corner. To the school. Oh, I knew. I knew already. But maybe (please God!), maybe farther down the street there'd be two children standing bewildered at a curbside. There were not, of course. I drove back to the rubble heap.

Then a numb blur of events: police, firemen, people struggling with the debris. Identification. Arms around me. I was at the clinic. I was being driven home. I was in my living room again. My mother was there, and I was telling her and my two little boys what had happened. Mother was praying.

Suddenly, as I sat there in the living room, perhaps even in midsentence—I don't know how long it took—I was being lifted right out of the room, lifted above it all, high into the sky, and placed by a beautiful gate. A cluster of happy people stood within the gate. In utter amazement I began recognizing the youthful, robust faces: Dad, my favorite aunt, Grandpa . . . and in the center of them all, the radiant form of Jesus! As I watched, He stretched out

His hands to welcome a child who was approaching, a smiling boy dressed in what seemed to be an unbleached muslin tunic over long trousers of the same homespun-looking fabric. Travis ran forward and grasped the hand of Jesus, looking up at Him with eager brown eyes. The cluster of people welcomed my son, and he seemed to recognize them, although some he had never met. As the joyful group turned to leave, Travis suddenly turned his shining face toward me.

"It's really neat here, Mommy."

"I know, Babe." My throat felt choked, and I don't know whether I spoke aloud or not.

"I really like it here."

"I know."

"Mommy . . . I don't want to go back."

"It's okay, Babe." And it was okay, in that transcendent moment. Nothing I could ever do, nothing that could ever happen here on earth, could make Travis as happy as I saw him right then. When I looked around me, I was back in my home.

That's where the long battle of grief was fought, of course: in the kitchen with its empty chair, in the bedroom where he'd said his good-night prayers, in the yard where he'd played hide-and-seek. Transcendent moments do not last—not for us on earth. Three years have passed since the day of the earthquake, passed among the daily routines of cleaning, cooking, chauffeuring, praying.

But neither do such moments fade. That scene at heaven's threshold is as vivid in each detail today as in the measureless instant when I was allowed to see. I have been granted another glimpse since then, this time of Tara among a group of joyfully playing children, all dressed in those tuniclike garments. (I did not see Travis this time, nor anyone else I recognized.)

Tara's mother understands no better than I the why of a child's death, the why of heaven's glory. I know only that both are real, and that—when we hear the answer at last—it will start with the words "I love you."

Her Final Gift

Natalie Kalmus

*D*ON'T WORRY, but come as soon as you can," my sister Eleanor wired. At the time, I was in London working out problems with one of the British motion picture companies.

I felt a deep, numbing pang. I knew Eleanor had been ill for some time. Surely this was her gentle way of telling me the end was coming.

I could not accept it. Always radiating charm, friendliness and an inner happiness, my sister had been a wonderful inspiration to those close to her. She had that rare trait of always giving others a pat on the back, lifting their spirits and sending them off with a fresh outlook on life.

When she was first stricken by the most fearsome of medical enemies, the doctors had told her that her days were numbered. Knowing this had not made the slightest difference in her warm interest in people—nor in her deep abiding faith in the wonder of God.

But now she needed me. I returned to the States and hurried to Eleanor, expecting to find her in bed in great pain. Instead she was in the living room perched jauntily on the sofa, looking more like a schoolgirl of seventeen than an incurably ill woman.

"Natalie"—she held out her arms joyously—"I'm so happy now that you're here. We have so much to talk over." To anyone listening, it might have seemed that I'd dropped in for a casual call.

After Eleanor had retired for the night, the doctor drew me aside. "Mrs. Kalmus," he said, "I think that it will be a most trying experience for you if you stay here through to the end. I'm afraid that your sister's last hours will be an agony of pain."

Medically I knew he was right. Yet the radiance I noticed in my sister's face seemed somehow to refute his statement. The strange feeling swept over me that the strength of my sister's spirit could well triumph over her pain.

During the next few days I discovered that Eleanor was doing many things that baffled the doctors. They were preparing her for some grim final moments. She was ignoring their solemn suggestions and remedies. One night she had me sit down on the side of her bed.

"Natalie, promise me that you won't let them give me any drugs. I realize that they are trying to help relieve my pain, but I want to be fully aware of every sensation. I am convinced that death will be a beautiful experience."

I promised. Alone later, I wept, thinking of her courage. Then, as I tossed in bed on through the night, I realized that what I took to be a calamity, my sister intended to be a triumph.

One afternoon Eleanor, in the most airy and lighthearted manner, asked several friends to a dinner party that she, on the spur of the moment, decided to hold. I was stunned. But Eleanor grinned at me impishly in high spirits. The sight of the happiness in her face checked my objections.

On the night of the party, Eleanor dressed meticulously, concealing the pain I knew she felt. We helped her downstairs before the guests were to arrive. Sitting in a turquoise chair in her yellow evening gown, she sparkled with life and gaiety.

The party was a grand success; the guests were never once aware of the illness that my sister concealed so expertly. That night, however, when she was carried to bed, her deep physical weariness appeared on the surface. Then I realized that my sister knew this was her final social fling. She had planned it that way.

Days later, the final hour drew near. I had been at her bedside for hours. We had talked about many things, and always I marveled at her quiet, sincere confidence in eternal life. Not once did the physical torture overcome her spiritual strength.

"Dear kind God, keep my mind clear and give me peace," she had murmured over and over again during those last days.

We had talked so long that I noticed she was drifting off to sleep. I left her quietly with the nurse and retired to get some rest. A few minutes later I heard my sister's voice calling for me. Quickly I returned to her room. She was dying.

I sat on her bed and took her hand. It was on fire. Then she seemed to rise up in bed almost to a sitting position.

"Natalie," she said, "there are so many of them. There's Fred . . . and Ruth—what's she doing here? Oh, I know!"

An electric shock went through me. Ruth! Ruth was her cousin who had died suddenly the week before. But Eleanor had not been told of Ruth's sudden death.

Chill after chill shot up and down my spine. I felt on the verge of some powerful, almost frightening knowledge.

Her voice was surprisingly clear. "It's so confusing. So many of them!" Suddenly her arms stretched out as happily as when she had welcomed me! "I'm going up," she murmured.

Then she dropped her arms around my neck—and relaxed in my arms. The will of her spirit had turned final agony into rapture. As I laid her head back on the pillow, there was a warm, peaceful smile on her face.

This was my sister's inheritance to me: her final, beautiful gift. I had seen for myself how thin was the curtain between life and death. I had glimpsed part of the wonderful truth about everlasting life. Never again will death frighten me in any way.

Travel Plans

by Katherine Krahling

I CAN'T SAY MY SON'S QUESTION caught me completely off guard. "Mama, where will I go after I die?" I'd just tucked five-year-old Timmy into bed and kissed him good night. He was so quiet, I had thought he was already sleeping. He wasn't. Now he stared up at me from the pillow, his eyes alert and serious.

"You'll go to heaven," I said, "and be with Jesus."

"But how will I find heaven? I don't know where it is."

My sweet Timmy. "When the time comes, you won't have any trouble. Jesus will be there, and He'll show you the way."

I kissed Timmy on the forehead. He hugged me tighter than usual, but he seemed to accept my explanation and, when I switched off the light, I thought I could hear his sleepy breathing.

I've always tried to be honest with my son about death. I've never had a choice. Timmy was born with spina bifida, a birth defect that left him paralyzed from the chest down and with a host of medical problems. For as long as I can remember, the doctors have told us to get ready to lose him. How could a mother ever prepare herself for that?

Instead, I concentrated on doing everything I could to keep Timmy here with me. He needed constant medical attention, and he couldn't go anywhere without a wheelchair.

I was with him twenty-four hours a day, always on the lookout for danger signs. Were his pupils dilated? Was he having trouble breathing? Was his pulse normal?

Getting Timmy ready for bed that night—like every night—had taken almost an hour. I gave him his medications, checked his IV tube, drained his catheter, tested his reflexes, massaged him with lotion. Even the slightest mistake could be serious.

Before I climbed into bed, I opened my door so I could hear Timmy down the hall. I had to be ready for any emergency.

I switched on my reading light and picked up a book. Suddenly a loud sob shattered the silence.

Timmy! I jumped to my feet and dashed down the hall to his room. He was lying right where I'd left him, crying.

"What's the matter, baby?" I asked, taking him gently in my arms. "Do you feel okay?"

He nodded but kept on sobbing, his little body shaking. Was it something serious? I felt his forehead. Normal. Timmy choked back his tears.

"Why are you crying?"

"I don't think I can go to heaven," he said at last.

"Why not?"

"Because my wheelchair won't fit into that box they send you in," he said. "How can I get to heaven without my wheelchair?"

I was relieved. I could handle this. I thought fast.

"You don't have to worry," I told him. "You won't need your wheelchair. You'll be able to walk and run, just like other boys."

"My legs will work?" he asked.

"That's right," I said, "and you'll have wings. You'll fly."

His eyes widened. "Really?"

"Really. The angels will bring you wings, when the time comes. And that's how you'll get to heaven. You can leave that old wheelchair behind!"

He buried his head in my arm, and I rubbed his back until I felt him relax. I gave him a few extra kisses and laid him down on the pillow. Then I tiptoed out of his room and back into my own bed.

I shut out the lights but lay there a long time. I'd just done a good bit of mothering, I knew that. But it was easy to explain death to a five-year-old. How could I understand it myself? My story about angel's wings might have been enough to comfort Timmy—but did he really know what death meant? Did he realize I wouldn't be there to care for him?

The thought of leaving Timmy alone, even in heaven, terrified me. *Lord, I just want to take care of my son. How can I do that if You take him from me?*

I rolled over and squeezed my eyes shut. Then I sat up. Timmy was crying again. I hurried down to his room.

"What's wrong, honey?" I whispered, sitting on the edge of his bed. He reached up and clung to me, but he didn't speak. "Tell me," I said. "What is it?"

He buried his head in my shoulder. Then he looked up and said, "Mama, I don't know how to fly."

I leaned back and stared at his face. To Timmy, those angel's wings weren't just a story. They were real. He wasn't worried about whether or not he would get them, but only how to use them when he did. That's how strong his faith is.

Timmy knew that God would take care of him. And when the time came, if the time came for me to let go, God would give me my own set of wings. I wrapped Timmy in my arms. We would be separated—but not forever. And someday we both would fly together.

When Angels Have No Names

by Joan Wester Anderson

*A*S A JOURNALIST AND AUTHOR I've reported on countless stories of angels. It's important to me that each of these
stories is checked out as thoroughly as possible. I like to
talk to the witness directly, and if there's corroboration,
such as newspaper clips or onlookers or medical reports,
I'll use them as well.

But there are moments when I'm unprepared: Someone
approaches me at a book signing when I have neither
notepad nor tape recorder, or phones in on a radio show
where I am a guest, or speaks up at a lecture, to tell a story
of her own. Invariably, during the hubbub these people get
away before I am able to jot down their full names and
addresses. But their stories are too good to go untold. I may
not have all their names right, but the facts are exactly as
they were related to me.

During a book signing in Lexington, Kentucky, a group of
women gathered around my table to tell about their neighbor, Barbara, who had not been able to come and tell me

this story herself. Barbara was driving her six-year-old son, Benjamin, to his piano lesson. They were late, and Barbara was beginning to think she should have canceled it. There was always so much to do, and Barbara, a night-duty nurse at the local hospital, had recently worked extra shifts. She was tired. The sleet storm and icy roads added to her tension. Maybe she should turn the car around.

"Mom!" Ben cried. "Look!"

Just ahead a car had lost control on a patch of ice. As Barbara tapped the brakes, the other car spun wildly, rolled over, and then crashed sideways into a telephone pole.

Barbara pulled over, skidded to a stop and threw open her door. Thank goodness she was a nurse—she might be able to help these unfortunate passengers. Then she paused. What about Ben? She couldn't take him with her —little boys shouldn't see scenes like the one she anticipated. But was it safe to leave him alone? What if their car were hit from behind? For a brief moment, Barbara considered going on her way. Someone else was sure to come along. No! "Ben, honey, promise me you'll stay in the car!"

"I will, Mommy," he said as she ran, slipping and sliding, toward the crash site.

It was worse than she'd feared. Two girls of high school age were in the car. One, the blonde on the passenger side, was dead, killed on impact. The driver, however, was still breathing. She was unconscious and pinned in the wreckage. Barbara quickly applied pressure to the wound in the teenager's head while her practiced eye catalogued the other injuries. A broken leg, maybe two, along with probable internal bleeding. But if help came soon, the girl would live.

A trucker had pulled up and was calling for help on his cell phone. Soon Barbara heard the ambulance sirens. A few moments later, she surrendered her lonely post to rescue workers. "Good job," one said as he examined the driver's wounds. "You probably saved her life, ma'am."

Perhaps. But as Barbara walked back to her car, a feeling of sadness overwhelmed her, especially for the family of the girl who had died. Their lives would never be the same. *O God, why do such things have to happen?*

Slowly Barbara opened her car door. What should she tell Benjamin? He was staring at the crash site, his blue eyes huge. "Mom," he whispered, "did you see it?"

"See what, honey?" she asked.

"The angel, Mom! He came down from the sky while you were running to the car. And he opened the door, and he took that girl out."

Barbara's eyes filled with tears. "Which door, Ben?"

"The passenger side. He took the girl's hand, and they floated up to heaven together."

"What about the driver?"

Ben shrugged. "I didn't see anyone else."

Later Barbara was able to meet the families of both victims. They expressed their gratitude for the help she had provided. Barbara was able to give them something more: Ben's vision. There was no way he could have known —by ordinary means—who was in the car or what had happened to either of the passengers. Nor could the passenger door have been opened; Barbara had seen its tangle of immovable steel herself. Yet Ben's account brought consolation to a grieving family. Their daughter was safe in heaven. And they would see her again.

PART VI

Recovery from Grief

You number my wanderings;
Put my tears into Your bottle;
Are they not in Your book?. . .
I will render praises to You,
For You have delivered my soul from death.
Have you not delivered my feet from falling,
That I may walk before God
In the light of the living?

Psalm 56:8, 13 NKJV

HEARING A STRIKING or favorite piece of music—the right tune at the right time. Planning a memorial ritual. Taking a pen in hand and writing a letter to a departed loved one. Finding a significant coin on the ground. Such acts can prompt emotional breakthroughs. They jolt us into a new realization: that God, who is trustworthy to safeguard our tears, is giving us new strength to walk toward "the light of the living." Sometimes these healing moments take us by surprise; sometimes we sense the need to give grace a space to work, maybe by commemorating an anniversary, as did

Andrew Lorenz or Carole Campbell. If you're saying, "Well, that's beyond my ability right now," just try looking for little graces, pennies on the sidewalk, shells on the beach. Like Aletha Jane Lindstrom, you might sense a rising gladness you haven't "felt for a long time."

Jesus Has a Rocking Chair

by Kathe Wunnenberg

God, am I supposed to hurt this much?" I sobbed as I looked at the teddy bear sitting in my rocking chair. "I miss my baby. Where is he now?"

Though often it seemed that God responded to my pleas with silence, that day God answered and encouraged me in an unexpected way. *It's probably another sympathy card*, I thought, as I ripped open the envelope. Although I appreciated receiving cards and letters, today was one of those times in my grief journey when I couldn't concentrate.

I felt relieved when I saw the cassette tape and a hand-scribbled note from my cousin Crystal. Words through song had been Crystal's gift to others since her youth when she and a troop of cousins performed together in homemade matching dresses and 1960s hairstyles as the Homanettes gospel group.

After several years our family ensemble dissolved, but Crystal and her sister Debbie continued music ministry together until Debbie died of cancer. In spite of her pain and loss, Crystal chose to press on and continue singing.

Her courage, perseverance and ability to view her personal difficulties as the bass notes in her life's song inspired me through the years.

Though distance has separated us for most of our lives, God has enabled Crystal and me to stay close in spirit, heart and prayer. I sensed this tape was one more way God would intertwine our lives.

My curiosity mounted as I slapped the tape into the cassette deck. Music filled the air, but I wasn't expecting what came next. I felt as if Crystal was sitting next to me, singing to my broken heart. Her words rang out, "He's the best parent a child could have. . . . Don't worry about the children, Jesus has a rocking chair. . . ."

As I pictured my child in the arms of Jesus being rocked back and forth on the heavenly throne, peace penetrated my soul. Though I had never pondered a divine rocking chair before and had no evidence from Scripture that this was true, I did know that God was in control and could do anything, including using these timely lyrics to encourage me.

I sensed God's presence and compassion for me in a personal, powerful way that day. Each time I listen to Crystal's tape, He continues to remind me that He loves and cares about every question I have about my loss. God is my Comforter and continues to use music to soothe my questioning soul.

Maybe it's time you, too, allowed Him to comfort you through music. And while you're listening, why not picture yourself sitting on Jesus' lap. Feel His arms wrap tightly around you as you lay your head on His shoulder. Then He begins to rock . . . and rock . . . and rock.

McKay's Pennies

by Paulette Everett

cKay, our only child, loved pennies. He loved life. When he was little, my husband Carl and I called him "couch hopper," because he was so active and fun loving that he'd often jump over our couch in sheer excitement. No matter what he did—whether it was climbing a tree, reading a book or saying his prayers—he did it full speed ahead.

He was especially intense about his faith. When he was still very young, we started to teach him to say thank you. Once when we prompted him, asking if he remembered what we called the two special words, he looked up at us with big eyes and said, "A-men!" At night he asked me to play "Surely the Presence of the Lord..." on the piano before he went to bed.

His passion for pennies started in the first grade, when his grandmother gave him a large pickle jarful. McKay carried it to school in his backpack for show-and-tell. After that, he was always on the lookout for pennies. When we went for a walk or to the store, he kept one eye peeled for a flash of copper and exhorted me to do likewise. It became a kind of ongoing family project to find pennies with McKay.

As he grew, so did his interest in spiritual things. He enjoyed Sunday school and church and playing hymns on the piano at home. When he was eleven, we sent him to summer camp at Laity Lodge, in the Texas Hill Country. Practically the first thing he told me when he returned was, "Mom, I've had a religious experience." He didn't have to say anymore; I could tell he had truly been moved.

McKay was twelve that September evening when Carl and I went to a business meeting. Carl called later to check on him, but there was no answer. "I'll go home and look in on him," Carl said. He thought McKay might have fallen asleep in front of the television set. But Carl became frightened as soon as he saw the back door of our house ajar. He dashed inside calling for McKay. The phone rang. It was someone demanding half a million dollars for our son's safe return.

We collected money to meet the kidnapper's demands. Then we waited for further instructions. We would have given anything to get McKay back, even our own lives, but it was not to be. Several days after his abduction, police found McKay's body in neighboring Louisiana. Eventually they arrested his killer. We believe McKay had been lured from our house by a man who claimed that Carl and I had been injured in an accident. The man forced our son into the trunk of his car and drove him to Louisiana. McKay made desperate attempts to escape and eventually the man shot him.

As sudden as a bolt of lightning, tragedy shattered our lives. There is no pain like the loss of a child, no grief so wrenching. What reason did I have to go on?

In the following weeks, life was a gray, featureless landscape I walked through in a stupor of pain. I wandered around our house begging God for comfort I didn't really believe existed. Fending off apathy, I forced myself through my daily routine. One morning I was about to pull out of the driveway to run an errand when I realized I'd forgotten my sunglasses and went inside the house to grab them. When I got back in the car, a coppery flash caught my eye. There on the armrest was a single, shiny penny catching the sunlight just so. I wrapped my hand around it and held it tight, not sure whether to cry or smile.

I thought no more about it until a few days later, when I noticed another penny on our porch, right in front of the door. I smiled. Was this a sign that McKay's spirit was still with us?

All afternoon I thought about the mysterious pennies. That night I said to Carl, "I know this sounds weird, but I think McKay's been here."

Carl looked at me. "Why?"

"He's leaving pennies." I showed him one.

We didn't discuss it any further. Then one of McKay's classmates called the house. "Miss Paulette," Ryan said, "I found four pennies in front of my locker. I'm sure McKay left them there."

That night I told Carl. "McKay can't come down from heaven," Carl said gently. I knew that, of course. *But angels can!* I thought.

Every time hope seemed out of reach, a penny turned up. Once, unable to eat anything at the table where McKay used to sit, I fled alone to a drive-in burger joint. Waiting dismally for my order, I glanced at the stainless-steel food tray. Four pennies were there where none had been just a few seconds before.

And so it went. McKay loved to read and be read to. He had hundreds of books—novels, histories, the classics—and we felt they should be donated to a good library. Our first thought was local Montgomery College. We toured the campus with its president, Dr. Bill Law, but we were having trouble coming to a decision. Then, outside the administration building, I spotted another shiny penny. "Dr. Law," I said, "your library will be the perfect place for McKay's books."

Most startling of all was what happened to my sister Pam, one of McKay's favorite people. He loved to visit her on her Mississippi farm, and she was devastated by his murder. One day, the summer after his death, Pam rolled the family Jeep, avoiding a stalled truck in the road. Miraculously she survived with minor injuries. As she was brought into the emergency room, she asked the nurse to remove her shoes. "There's gravel in there or something," she complained.

By now you can probably guess it wasn't gravel. Two pennies fell out, one from each shoe. Later Pam told me that a strange force seemed to push her back into her seat while the Jeep was flipping over, keeping her from being thrown from the vehicle.

I know what that force is. It is God's love, shown to us through friends, the Bible, prayers and pennies from angels. It's what I found when I thought nothing could ever comfort me again.

While the Sun Comes Up

by Patricia Lorenz

$\mathcal{I}$T WAS A DILEMMA I hadn't expected. On the day before the second anniversary of my ex-husband's death, our eleven-year-old son Andrew came to me with an odd request for honoring his memory.

"Mom, I've got it all planned," Andrew said. "I want you and me to go out to the lake and sit and think about Dad while the sun comes up. We'll take along cherry Jell-O with sliced bananas in it. That's what Dad liked. We used to make it when I'd see him on weekends. Okay, Mom?"

It wasn't exactly okay. I still had hurt feelings about Harold. I was still bitter about the way our marriage had ended, how he'd filed for the divorce without any effort at marriage counseling, how he'd remarried the week our divorce was final. No, this would be too awkward.

"Andrew, it's October; it's supposed to be really cold tomorrow. Couldn't you just think about your dad at home?"

"Mom, please. We can wear long underwear and take a blanket."

I thought I'd done a good job of helping Andrew adjust to his father's death, and I was determined to be the best "only" parent a child could have. But I was unprepared for something like this. As Andrew waited for my reply, the pleading look on his face told me how much this would mean to him.

"All right, Andrew. We'll have to get up at 5:15 if you want to get there while it's still dark."

"No problem, Mom! I'll set my alarm. Do you think Wayne would come if I asked him?"

I wondered what Wayne, the man I'd been dating for three months, would think about Andrew's plan. Wayne's wife had died just two months after Harold, and I was sure that Wayne was still dealing with his own grief. I didn't know if it was fair to drag him along to Andrew's strange beach ceremony.

That afternoon, when Wayne stopped by the house, Andrew explained his plan and said he'd like the three of us to be together. "So, Wayne, do you want to go?"

I shot Wayne a look that said something like, *Are you sure about this?* Then I said, "Do you realize it's going to be only twenty degrees tomorrow morning? With the wind off the lake, the windchill factor will probably be below zero!"

Wayne smiled. "Sure I want to go, Andrew. I'm glad you asked me."

Wayne arrived at our house at 5:40 the next morning, wearing full winter gear. I was wearing a jogging suit under my clothes, plus a heavy jacket and earmuffs. The Jell-O Andrew had made was retrieved from the refrigerator and the container put in a brown paper bag. Wayne tossed an old green bedspread into the van.

A few minutes later, in the pitch darkness, we arrived at Grant Park Beach in South Milwaukee, the only humans in sight. Wayne and Andrew smoothed out the bedspread on the sand, about thirty feet from the jet black water. We moved up close to the front of the bedspread and pulled the back half up around us as a windbreak.

Andrew had instructed us carefully beforehand that we would sit without talking. At first his silence rule made me uncomfortable. But then I looked at Wayne and Andrew and knew that they were both remembering and missing the person they had loved so much in life.

I knew Wayne was thinking about the wonderful relationship he'd had with Janet, his wife of thirty-one years. And without a doubt, Andrew was thinking about Harold. About the walks they often took along this lake. About the plays and concerts his father had taken him to.

I recalled the early days of our marriage. The bike rides, teaching Harold to ice-skate, the two wonderful trips to Arizona to visit his sister and brother and their families.

I remembered when Andrew was born, in Harold's

fifty-first year, and how proud he was of his new son. Why, he'd passed out cigars the day he found out I was pregnant!

I remembered how scared I was when Harold had emergency gallbladder surgery. And how I laughed when he dressed up in a crazy red-plaid sport coat and too-short orange-plaid pants for "nerd day" at the high school where he was principal.

Suddenly the unhappy times in our marriage faded away, and as I watched a new line of pink and steel blue clouds inching their way onto the horizon, I felt as if a dam had broken. All the good memories I'd buried the day Harold moved out of our home came rushing back.

I pulled the bedspread tighter around my neck and snuggled closer to Andrew, who had his head on my chest, trying to keep the cold away. The more I thought about Harold, the more I realized how much I missed him.

Even though it was still twenty minutes or so until sunrise, the intensity of sunlight from below the horizon was starting to fill the beach with an eerie sense of "almost" day. And I was being filled with an eerie sense of "almost" peace.

Andrew motioned that it was time to eat the Jell-O. I took the lid off the container. When I placed one of the plastic spoons into Wayne's hand, I squeezed his fingers through the bulky gloves. He smiled, and I knew he understood what was going on in my mind and in Andrew's.

So we ate red cherry Jell-O at dawn on the shore of Lake Michigan in a windchill that felt very close to zero degrees. But somehow I wasn't shivering. And the Jell-O tasted good.

Just as the sun popped up on the horizon in a magnificent display of color, Wayne and Andrew stood up.

"It's okay to talk now," Andrew said.

Wayne put his big arms around Andrew and held him close. "I know what you're going through, son. I loved my wife very much, just like you loved your dad. And it's a wonderful thing to take the time to cherish those memories. And Andrew, I don't think I told you how much I love red Jell-O with bananas!"

I stood up as the full ball of wild orange sun now rested precariously and breathtakingly beautiful above the horizon, and I said, "Andrew, let's walk along the shore for a minute."

"Good idea," Wayne said. "I'll go warm up the van."

So it was that Wayne and I were able to let an eleven-year-old child lead us into a strange world of ceremony and silence . . . and where we all, especially I, were able to grieve openly. Andrew and I faced the love we had for Harold Lorenz head-on and then moved ahead in a celebration of life that includes new love and wonderful warm feelings.

Little Dog Found

by Aletha Jane Lindstrom

I SAW HER FIRST IN MID-DECEMBER during one of Michigan's cruelest winters. She was running across the frozen barnyard, a small ghost of a dog, almost obliterated from sight by swirling snow.

Living in the country, we've become accustomed to seeing abandoned dogs and cats. We seldom see the same one twice, but this one was strangely different. My husband Andy and I glimpsed her frequently—in the barnyard, the fields, the woods, along the road. And she was running, always running, head held high, either trying desperately to find someone or fleeing in abject terror.

My heart went out to the small creature. How could she possibly survive the bitter cold? Even Collie, our big farm dog, who loves winter, was content to remain indoors.

But the plight of the little lost dog provided only brief distraction from the black mood that engulfed me. My dad had died recently, and it had been hard to let him go. Though I was sustained by God's promise that we'll be reunited with our loved ones, lately there had been dark times when my faith flickered. Could I trust God's promise?

The question gnawed at me. For a while I prayed about it; then stopped.

On one below-zero evening as I walked down the drive for the newspaper, I sensed I was being followed. I looked back, and there was the lost dog—a small beagle with big freckled feet, a wagging tail and soft, pleading eyes. I removed my mitten, but before I could touch her, she cowered and drew back. Then she panicked and fled to the woods, leaving bloody footprints in the snow.

I couldn't sleep that night; the memory of those eyes haunted me. Had she been stolen for hunting and later abandoned? Where was she now? Had she found shelter from the bitter cold, or was she still running, terrified and alone?

The next morning we followed tracks in the woods until we found her. Andy held out a piece of meat, and she crept toward it on her belly. When she drew close enough, I grabbed her. She struggled and cried until her strength was gone. Then she lay whimpering in my arms.

We wrapped her in a blanket and took her to the vet. "Poor little mutt," I said as we carried her in. "He'll probably have to put her down."

The vet removed the blanket, now bloodstained, and ran gentle, capable hands over the emaciated body. The head, it seemed, was permanently tipped to one side. She was covered with cuts, welts and scars, and the pads were worn from her feet. "She's either been running for days over frozen ground or digging to make a bed in the leaves—probably both," he said.

Silently we awaited the verdict. "She's a good little beagle," he said at last. "I think we can save her."

"Then I'd better advertise for the owner," I said.

"I wouldn't bother," the vet replied. "She's smart. If she's from around here, she'd have found her way home—that is, if she'd wanted to go. . . ."

"But she's so frightened. How long before she'll get over that?"

"Never—not entirely. Apparently she's been badly abused. When that happens, a dog becomes either vicious or afraid for the rest of its life." His voice softened. "And obviously this little dog will never be vicious."

"You mean she'll even be afraid of us?"

"Probably." He was silent for a moment and then added thoughtfully, "But we can't be sure. Sometimes love works wonders."

That night I brought a dog bed from the attic and placed it near the kitchen stove. To my surprise, she crept in immediately, settled down with a long sigh and closed her eyes. For the first time, the trembling stopped.

I knelt beside her, my mind filled with questions. This small stranger, seemingly from nowhere—why had she approached me in the drive, pleading for affection? And why, needing it so much, had she fled in terror when I offered it? It seemed we had something in common: We were both afraid to trust.

Gently I stroked the soft ears. "You can trust us, Puppy," I whispered. "You needn't be afraid, ever again." I placed an old shawl over her and tucked it in, making sure it would stay.

"It seems we have ourselves another dog," Andy said the next morning.

I nodded. "I'm not sure I'm happy about it. Now that Tim's away from home, I figured we wouldn't get another dog . . . after Collie. They all die and break your heart sooner or later." *That's the way with love*, I thought, remembering Dad.

"Let's forget the heartaches," Andy said gently, "and remember the happy times. They've given us so many of them."

He was right, of course. I couldn't imagine life without a dog. Besides, I'd already succumbed to this one. She was so hurt and frightened, so little and alone. And she needed us so desperately. Her eyes, her most endearing feature, were dark puddles, reflecting her emotions. I longed to see them shining with eagerness and love, as a little dog's eyes should be.

We continued calling her "Puppy." Somehow it seemed to fit. I remembered what the vet said about her fear, but I couldn't believe she'd be afraid of us. She was. She allowed us to minister to her injuries, but when we reached out to pet her, she cringed and pulled away, as if she feared we would strike her. I wondered if perhaps that was why her head was tipped.

We gave up trying to pet her. "She'll come to us when she's ready to trust us," I said. But the rejection hurt. I wondered if that's the way God feels about us when we fail to trust Him.

Andy, unaware of my thoughts, said, "She'll learn. It's a beagle's nature to be happy and affectionate."

"Love casteth out fear," I said, quoting 1 John 4:18 KJV. Here was another of God's promises. Could I believe this one?

Weeks passed and Puppy didn't respond. Collie seemed to be her only security. I usually walked Collie down the lane in late afternoon. When Puppy's paws were healed, she joined us. Sometimes she'd wander off, following a scent. But when she discovered she was alone, she'd race back to Collie.

Those were the good days. There were other, heartbreaking ones when the beagle seemed to be in a trance. She'd wander to the roadside and huddle there, a solitary figure, gazing up and down. I'd send Collie to bring her back. Inside she took to her bed, her eyes confused and unseeing. I'd sit by her and slip my hand under her chin. "Is there someone you love, Puppy? Someone you've been searching for?"

At such times I wished I knew where she'd come from, what she'd experienced. Then, looking at the sad eyes, the ugly scars, I decided I'd rather not know.

By late spring I noticed changes in her behavior. Her trips to the roadside grew fewer, and she waited as impatiently as Collie for our walks. There were times, too, when we were petting Collie, that she'd draw close and watch wistfully. And that was the way things remained.

Then one September afternoon I leaned on the back fence, watching our two dogs. They were in the far side of a back field, engaged in a recently discovered pastime: chasing grasshoppers. Collie hunted with her eyes, leaping on her prey. Puppy hunted with her nose, snuffling along the ground. Only her waving white-tipped tail was visible above the weeds.

I watched in amusement. The little dog had been with us eight months now, but she was still afraid, still wouldn't come to be petted. Despite our hopes, our prayers, love hadn't worked its magic after all. Yet just having the small dog and knowing she was enjoying life lent pleasure to my days.

Collie saw me and came running. I knelt and put my arms around her, my eyes still on the waving white-tipped tail moving in the maze of weeds. Suddenly Puppy discovered she was alone. She darted in frantic circles until she caught Collie's scent. Then she came racing toward us.

When she reached us, she pushed her eager, squirming

body between Collie and me. She looked up, her eyes shining with that soft light that comes only from the heart. "Me too!" they plainly said. "Love me too!"

"I do love you, Puppy. I'll always love you," I said, snuggling her close. So love had cast out fear, just as the promise says. "It's all right, Dad," I whispered. A gladness was rising in me that I hadn't felt for a long time. I knew then that God is faithful to all His promises.

A Perfect Heart

by Barbara Laporte

*P*HIL AND I LOVED THE BEACH. We'd go every year. Florida, Puerto Vallarta, Maui. "Hon, we need a break from this Minnesota cold," he'd always say. We'd stroll the shore, covering the sand with footprints and watching them fill with water. We'd get up early to watch the sunrise and hunt for seashells all morning. I even had a special place to display all the beach stuff we brought home. The top of a bedroom dresser was filled with seashells. One piece stood out from the rest: a heart-shaped shell. Phil and I had picked it up while on a Valentine's Day getaway to South Padre Island, Texas. It was so solid and round. So perfect. So one-of-a-kind. "Phil," I said, pulling it out of the wet sand. "Look at this!"

"Well, isn't that something!" Phil said. "Hey, happy Valentine's Day!"

Then he wrapped me in his arms. I felt so warm and good I wanted this moment to last forever. I thought life with Phil would always be this wonderful.

But it wasn't. Phil started losing weight. He couldn't eat his favorite foods. One day he was so sick I drove him to the emergency room. He stayed in the hospital for a week. When the doctor operated, he found an abdominal tumor. He called us to his office for a final prognosis. "Phil, you have stomach cancer," he said. "It's just a matter of time."

That night Phil and I sat silently on the living room couch. I couldn't look at him. I was so afraid I was going to break down.

Finally my husband spoke. "It'll be okay, Barbara," he said, taking my hand and looking into my eyes.

"What am I going to do without you, Phil?" I could barely get the words out.

Phil pulled me close. "I'll always be with you," he said. "In your heart."

Then one month later, Phil died. I brought the heart-shaped shell to his wake at the chapel. Everyone gathered in a circle. "When you get the shell, it's your turn to share a few words about Phil," I said. Everyone had a special story to tell. When the shell was passed to the last person in the circle, it broke in half. *Fitting*, I thought. My heart was broken too.

The days after Phil's funeral were busy: paying off hospital bills, writing thank-you cards. Friends came by with casseroles and flowers. All the activity smothered my grief.

But then it stopped, and I had to face the pain. Face being without Phil. I fell into a deep, bottomless grief. Finally my sister arranged for us to go to Hawaii. "I can't," I said, but I was too despondent to put up much resistance.

The moment I stepped on the beach, I felt the sadness rush in all over again, like the rising waves washing away footprints in the sand. *I can't walk on the beach without Phil, Lord. Will I ever feel whole again?* The sea spray stung my face ever so slightly. I felt an urge to look down. And there I saw it, glimmering in the foam of a receding wave. A heart, half-buried in the sand. A perfect heart.

Golden Memories

by Carole Campbell

O N THAT EARLY AUTUMN AFTERNOON, it was my turn to host a group of us widows who met for lunch on a regular basis. Today everyone was trying to cheer me up. "Carole, this is absolutely your best chicken salad ever," my friend Betty declared. Helen quickly added, "I can't wait to taste that cream cake." As I sliced into the moist layers, everyone clapped, but I had to force myself to smile.

You have to stop thinking about it, I told myself. Since my husband Bill died, I'd endured two wedding anniversaries without him. But now our fiftieth was coming up on October 7, and grief pulled at me like an undertow.

"I know your golden anniversary is around the corner," Betty said quietly. "You need to go somewhere. Try to distract yourself with someplace you've always wanted to see."

"I'll try, Betty."

But I didn't have the energy to go away. When October 7 came, I ate dinner in front of the TV in our family room. Sadly, I reached for the big photo album on the coffee table and opened the worn velveteen cover. I stared down at the pictures, some yellowing beneath the plastic pages. There were Bill and I when we first started dating. My thoughts traveled back to the night we met at the skating rink. We skated every single number together, and I could still feel his strength as I leaned back into his arms. We were perfect partners.

I flipped to the photos of us in front of our house on the day our mortgage was approved, then of me cradling our newborn son. Image after image brought back a flood of memories. But mostly I stared at the black-and-white snapshot of Bill and me coming down the steps moments after we'd been married in a simple service at the Seventh Avenue Baptist Church in Huntington, West Virginia. The orchid on my Bible, I remembered, had doubled as the corsage for my suit after the ceremony.

Bill and I moved away from Huntington, and I hadn't been back to the church for years. I'd heard they'd renovated it. Tears sprang to my eyes as I tried to push the memories aside. *I've got to forget all this*, I told myself firmly. *These memories just hurt too much.*

I shut the album with a snap and started to get up when suddenly the thought crossed my mind. *Stop trying to forget. Go back to that church where it all began, and remember.*

I couldn't get the idea out of my head. It seemed rash to barge into a church that I didn't belong to. Yet as I lay in bed that night, a plan formed. Tomorrow was Sunday. The church was about ten miles away across the Ohio River.

I could slip in quietly, say a prayer in Bill's memory and go home. No one would even notice that I was there. Maybe it would make me feel better.

It's not like me to act impulsively, but the next morning I got in the car and drove off to the neighborhood I remembered from so long ago. I parked and walked down the block to the church. Keeping my head down, I slipped quietly into a pew in the back of the sanctuary.

What am I doing here? Maybe I should just get back in the car and drive home.

"Hello!" A woman about my age came up and extended her hand. "I don't think I've seen you before," she said. "Is this the first time you've been to our church?"

"Well, no, I was married here. Yesterday was my fiftieth wedding anniversary," I explained, feeling awkward. "My husband died two years ago."

"And you've come back to celebrate all your years together—that's wonderful!"

Celebrate? The idea of celebrating certainly hadn't entered my mind.

More people walked up to me and introduced themselves, and then the pastor himself came over. "Mrs. Campbell? One of the ladies just told me why you're here. We think it's wonderful you and your husband had so many happy years together. Would you mind if I told the rest of the congregation about it?"

The word *wonderful* hadn't occurred to me either. Of

course it's true, my life with Bill had been wonderful. Suddenly I thought of his face lighting up at one of the jokes we had shared and remembered the many good times we had had together hiking and camping along the river. Just the two of us.

The service began, and I was caught up in the familiar old hymns. We sang "Savior, like a shepherd lead us, much we need Thy tender care," one of Bill's favorites. I thought of his booming voice and the way our fingers touched when we held the hymnal together, how natural and right it felt to be together.

Then the pastor pointed toward me. "I'd like everyone to welcome a special guest. Mrs. Campbell married Bill Campbell in our church fifty years ago. Bill has gone to heaven, but Carole is with us today to celebrate their union."

Celebrate. All heads turned to me. For an instant I felt myself walking down the aisle again on Bill's arm, holding tight, and looking into his kind brown eyes as we took our vows.

When the service ended, I was surrounded by well-wishers wanting to know more about Bill's and my life together. I told them about our sons and grandchildren, about all the many blessings and challenges Bill and I had shared for better and for worse.

Finally I said good-bye to everyone and walked down the church steps just as I had fifty years ago with Bill.

Decades had passed but the essence of our relationship would never change. God had given us a rich and vibrant life together, a perfect partnership that needed to be not mourned but celebrated.

I couldn't wait to tell the girls when we got together next Wednesday.

PART VII

Journey to Forgiveness

Have mercy upon me, O God,
According to Your loving-kindness. . . .
A broken and a contrite heart—
These, O God, You will not despise.

Psalm 51:1, 17 NKJV

A JOURNEY TO FORGIVENESS can follow a long and wind-ing road, as evidenced by the variety of stories in this sec-tion. If we think about it, any number of "forgiveness situations" require us to call on God's intervening grace. This is a journey we can't make alone; we need divine help

- To forgive someone who is specifically or tangentially responsible for our loss, whether that person is a stranger or maybe even myself

- To forgive myself for some rudeness or unkindness for which I can't apologize because it's "too late"

- To receive assurance of God's forgiveness

- To forgive God for allowing a death and, as Jonnie Lauten Clemmons says, betraying my trust

The inspiring stories in this section lead us to the peace of God that can ease our pain of loss.

Front-Row Seat

by Dwayne Douglas

MY FATHER WAS AS STURDY and steadfast as the craggy West Virginia hills where we lived; like most sons, I viewed him as indestructible. That is why his death when I was a teen struck such a terrible blow—devastating particularly because I was convinced I was responsible.

Dad was a lathe operator at a brass foundry, whose ear-splitting whistle we could hear at quitting time even though the foundry was in the next town over. He came home from work soot-smeared and sweaty, brass chips glinting in his dark hair. After a shower he claimed his humble throne—a worn leatherette recliner in the family room—until Mom called us to supper. He never talked much until dessert, because he was usually so hungry. But then he laughed and joked with my brother Dana and me, and helped us with our homework while Mom cleaned up the dishes.

Dad hadn't gone far in school himself. Hard times forced him into the factory. But he had high hopes for his boys. He told me to reserve a front-row seat for him at graduation. It was going to be as big a day for him as it would be for me.

I loved Dad fiercely. Hard as he worked, he drove me to football practice and cheered at Friday-night games. Afterward Dad would throw his arm around me and say, "I'm proud of you, Dwayne," no matter if we had won or lost. One area where we differed, though, was religion. Dad was a true believer. But at an early age I had been exposed to a hellfire-and-damnation preacher at a church we attended just long enough to scare me off religion. Not that I didn't believe in God. I was just uncertain about the strength of my faith, so I didn't lean on it the way Dad did his. I didn't have much use for church.

One day during my senior year, Dad invited me along while he did some errands after work. "I'll drive us to Martinsburg; then you can take over on the way back." I had just acquired my permit and was thrilled about any chance to practice my driving.

When we started home, traffic was light. Dad laid a calloused hand on my forearm and said, "I'm proud of you, Son." Then he leaned back, a little like the way he relaxed in his easy chair. I hit a sharp curve. I don't remember what happened after that.

I woke up in an emergency room, a doctor leaning over me intently. "How's my dad?" I gasped, panicky. I think I tried to get up.

A nurse said, "I'm sorry, Dwayne," while slipping a needle into my arm. "He didn't make it." And again I was out.

Later, in intensive care, hooked up to what seemed like a million monitors and IV poles, my face and head swathed in bandages, in such pain that it even hurt to groan, I thought, *How can I ever forgive myself?*

Over and over my mother said, "Dwayne, you mustn't blame yourself." But every day I wished it had been me instead of him.

I missed the funeral. I came home to the season's last few leaves drifting like parachutes onto our green roof. The house seemed so empty without him. Through a window, the dusty afternoon light suffused his chair, just as he left it. I stared at the impression his head had left after years of his leaning back. Empty, empty, empty.

I glanced at a sympathy card on the table: "And God shall wipe away all tears. . . ." If only it were true.

Somehow I made it through senior year. Three new friends kind of adopted me and invited me to a Friday-night youth group at their church. I couldn't bring myself to go at first, but soon I gave in to the idea of asking God to help me forgive myself. Where else could I turn but to where Dad had turned?

Then came graduation. "Save me a front-row seat," he had said. How could I even walk across that stage? When my name was called, I hurried, head down, wanting to get it over with. But before I reached the table where the diplomas were arrayed, I felt slowed down. A tide of good feeling surged through me, a relief and sense of well-being such as I had never felt before. Then I experienced a kind of light shining through me, a complete sensation of healing and peace, full of love, acceptance, joy. I knew it was God, my Heavenly Father, wrapping me in forgiveness so I could forgive myself, and pouring reassurance into my life.

I looked out into the audience, half expecting to see Dad done up in his Sunday suit, hair slicked back, applauding until his palms were red. I saw Mom and Dana, beaming. And though I didn't see my father, I felt his love, as indestructible as the West Virginia hills.

He had his front-row seat after all.

What Forgiveness Brings

by Arna Washington

$\mathcal{I}$'D JUST SEEN MY GRANDSON Corrick off to school and was going through the mail when the return address on an official-looking envelope jumped out at me. Texas Department of Criminal Justice. Every three years I'd received a letter from them. "Dear Arna Washington," it invariably read. "This is to inform you that offender Ronald Dwayne Flowers, ID#00393525, is up for parole. If you wish to protest. . . ."

And every time I saw those words, a bitter flame rekindled inside me. If I wished to protest? Ron Flowers killed my daughter. He destroyed my family, my whole life. He deserved to rot in prison. As long as I had breath left in my body, I'd make sure that was where he stayed. You're darn right I protested!

I sat on the couch and slowly opened the letter, feeling as if I were opening an old wound. Thinking about my daughter's senseless death still hurt, even after fourteen years. "Dear Arna Washington," I read. "This is to inform you that under the Mandatory Release Program, offender Ronald Dwayne Flowers, ID#00393525, will soon be released. If you have questions. . . ." There had to be some mistake! Will be released? How could that man be getting out? How could he be getting a chance to start over when my beautiful Deirdra never would?

I looked away from the letter, my eyes stinging with angry tears. All around me, lining the walls and on end tables, were pictures of my daughter, a record of her too-short life—from the chubby-cheeked baby who instantly won her big brother Derek's heart to the tall young woman who became a teacher, following in her father Marcellus' and my footsteps. I picked up the last photo I had of my daughter, her face lit up with a smile, her arms around her kindergarten students, as sweet and trusting as they were. That was DeDe: all about giving, all about love.

Until a killer took her from us. That terrible night in February 1984, the phone jolted me awake. It was Carlton, a guy DeDe had met recently. They were supposed to be out on their second date. Instead, he was yelling, "Deirdra's been shot! She's at Ben Taub!"

Marcellus and I raced to the hospital. The bullet had ripped through DeDe's brain, and the doctors told us there was no hope. Only machines were keeping her alive.

We never left her side. "Come on, baby, fight," I urged, squeezing her hand, praying that somehow my love could bring her back. But around six in the morning, DeDe gave a little sigh, and she was gone. I kissed her cheek for the last time and vowed, "I won't rest, baby. Not until I get the person who did this to you." We buried DeDe on what would have been her twenty-seventh birthday.

Details about the killing were sketchy. The police said she'd been in the seediest part of Houston, in front of an apartment building crawling with drug dealers, when she was shot. I told the officers there was no way our daughter, whose friends used to tease her about being more innocent than her kindergartners, would even have known such a place existed. When they questioned Carlton, he admitted he'd taken her there—to collect a debt, he claimed. A couple of men jumped him and beat him up. In the scuffle, someone shot DeDe.

The police arrested Ron Flowers for her murder. I couldn't wait for our day in court. "I'm going to look that man in the face and let him know exactly what he's done," I said to my husband. "And then I'm going to ask the judge to put him away forever." But Flowers pleaded guilty. There would be no trial, no chance for me to confront the man who killed my daughter. And no justice, I decided when I learned his sentence: only thirty-five years in prison.

Thirty-five years couldn't begin to make up for DeDe's life. Or for the devastation her murder wreaked on our family. Without her love, it was as if we didn't know how to live anymore. Derek, who'd been so close to his baby sister, broke down completely and developed serious kidney problems. Marcellus was paralyzed with grief. He could hardly function in front of his classroom. Being around all those young people reminded him too much of what he'd lost. Finally he took early retirement.

On the outside I was able to go on. I went to church, went back to my job as a reading teacher. Inside I struggled as much as my husband and son did. I kept looking at DeDe's picture and talking to her as if that might keep her with me, begging God to let me hear her voice one more time. I tried to make sense of what had happened. No matter how hard I prayed, the answers didn't come.

With the birth of Derek's son Corrick, my grief began to fade. But my anger toward Ron Flowers did not. Not that there was much I could do except make sure he stayed behind bars. I did see to it, though, that the drug den where DeDe was killed was shut down. No more innocent young people would die there.

That sense of satisfaction paled when Derek died of kidney failure. Then Marcellus died. A heart attack, doctors said, but I knew what really killed him was having both his children go before their time. In the space of ten years, my immediate family was wiped out, and all I could think was *Ron Flowers did this to us!*

I'd retired by then. I was raising Corrick, and I threw myself into his activities at church, school, Boy Scouts. He was all I had left. Still, anger burned deep inside me.

I crumpled the letter from the Department of Criminal Justice and sank back onto the couch, those long-held feelings leaping to the surface like flames licking hungrily at tinder. "Lord, You know why I'm angry," I cried. "I've struggled to accept that nothing is going to bring my baby back. But accept that the man who killed her is going free? You're asking too much!" I resolved once more to forget about Ron Flowers. I might not be able to keep him in prison; at least I could keep him out of my life.

But he just wouldn't leave my thoughts. At our annual church conference several weeks later, a prison choir performed. The men didn't look mean and hard, as I'd assumed criminals would. Then my pastor, Rev. Homer Williams, announced he was serving as a mentor at Jester II's InnerChange Freedom Initiative, a Prison Fellowship program nearby. Before I knew it, I was asking, "Pastor, next time you're there, can you see if they know of a Ron Flowers?"

My pastor called a few days later. "The young man you're looking for is in the InnerChange program."

Ron Flowers was only twenty miles from my home?

Apparently he'd accepted God into his life, and his counselor, the director of the program, wanted to talk with me about him, my pastor said. "Ron's a changed man," the director told me a few days later. "He'd like to get in touch with you."

"I don't want anything to do with him!" I protested. "I don't care how much he's changed!" But I couldn't stop thinking about him. Finally I agreed to allow Ron Flowers to write me.

Within days I received a letter. Not once did he apologize or show any remorse. How dare he! I was so furious I refused to answer his letter.

Yet I found myself going with my district United Methodist Church Prison Fellowship ministry to visit Jester II. As we toured the library, I noticed a young man huddled in a corner. I knew instinctively it was Ron Flowers. I had to leave the room.

As soon as I got home, I wrote him back: "That letter was totally inappropriate. Not only did you murder my daughter, you destroyed my whole family!" I sent him the program from DeDe's funeral, with her picture and a tribute a friend had written to "Our Deirdra." I figured I'd never hear from him again.

But I did. "Dear Mrs. Washington," Ron Flowers wrote. "As soon as I mailed that letter, I knew it was not right. I am so sorry for what I did to your family. I know you must have questions for me, and I'd like to answer them face-to-face. I pray you'll give me that chance."

For years I had wanted to confront this man, to make sure he understood the anguish he'd caused. After Corrick went to bed that night, I paced the living room, going over the photos of my daughter, one by one. "Baby, I want to do right by you," I whispered, "but I know I need to move on." Then to God I pleaded, "Isn't there any way I can do both?"

I decided the only answer was to see Ron Flowers. Once I heard what he had to say, maybe I would be able to put all the pain and anger behind me. Through my pastor and the prison director, we set up a meeting.

Last October 13, I got up early, fixed Corrick his breakfast as usual and took him to school. *I want some closure,* I thought as I headed to the prison with my pastor. *But, Lord, I'm going to need Your help.*

In the Jester II meeting room, my pastor showed me to a seat at the table and then moved back to give me some privacy. The door opened. A young man in prison whites entered the room. He walked toward me slowly, clutching a Bible, and sat opposite me. I noticed his hands were shaking as badly as mine.

"I'm Arna Washington."

"I'm Ron," he replied, so softly I had to lean forward to hear him.

There was an awkward silence. Then I asked the question only he could answer. "What happened that night?"

He let out his breath and began. "This guy Carlton came into the apartment. He wanted drugs but didn't have money. My friends started beating on him. He ran downstairs, and I grabbed a gun and went after him. When the car he came in started driving off, I panicked. I shot into the car window." Ron's hand clenched his Bible. "I never meant to hurt your daughter, Mrs. Washington. I'm sorry."

I didn't know what to say, but I couldn't let out all my emotions in front of this stranger. As a defense, I went into my teacher mode. "Young man, life on the outside is going to be tough. You can't hang onto that Bible every minute when you get out of here," I said sharply. "You're going to have to carry the Lord inside you—"

Forgive him, Mom. DeDe! I'd know her voice anywhere.

Had anyone else heard? I glanced around. My pastor was sitting quietly in one corner, the prison director in another. Ron was silently waiting for me to finish.

Those words had been meant for me alone. That was all God had my baby tell me. But it was enough. I pushed back my chair and got up. "Come here, son," I said.

Warily Ron stood, and then came around to my side of the table.

I reached out my arms. He took a step forward. Then we were holding each other, weeping together, the tears putting out the last bitter embers inside me, washing away the anger I'd been carrying for too long, and letting the love of the Lord fill its place.

When we moved apart, I took a good look at Ron. And I saw the person he'd been fourteen years before—a mixed-up young man who didn't know what he was doing when he shot my daughter; who'd probably caused his mother no end of worry.

"Ron, this may be hard for you to believe," I said, "but I want to forgive you. I want to be at peace with you."

Ron's eyes filled again. He squeezed my hand tightly. "I want that too," he murmured.

I knew Deirdra would have wanted nothing less.

No Chance to Say Good-bye

by Debra Lupien-Robillard

FOR WEEKS AFTER my little brother Billy died, I found I could remember the details of that day better than I could remember him. The burgers sizzling on the stove. The dust dancing in the sunlight. Even the clothes I was wearing. What loomed largest in my mind, though, was how horribly I had treated Billy that day. How could God have let me act that way when he knew it would be the last time I would ever speak to my brother?

It was a bright, warm April day. At eleven, the oldest, I was responsible for taking care of my little sister LeeAnne and my two younger brothers Billy and Jimmy until Mom and Dad came home from work. After school I usually did my homework and cleaned the house while I kept an eye on the kids.

That afternoon Billy didn't walk home with us. A lot of times he hung around school with his friends and came home later. But I always hurried LeeAnne and Jimmy so I could have supper started by the time Dad came in. That way I would have an entire hour alone with him to play word games or cards or simply talk.

I had just started the burgers when I heard Dad's foot-steps on the front porch. I grabbed a soda from the refrig-erator for him.

"Hi, pumpkin," Dad said, giving me a big hug. He took a swig of his soda. "How about some crazy eights?" We were deep into a competitive game when Billy called.

"Deb, I'm over at Johnny's, okay?"

"Why ask me?" I replied peevishly, annoyed at the intru-sion into my time with Dad. "I don't care what you do." I waited, braced for a confrontation. It didn't come.

"I already called Mom," he said calmly. "She said it was okay."

"Then why ask me?"

"I'm supposed to let you know, so you don't worry."

"Whatever," I snapped. "I've got to go."

"Bye, Debbie," Billy said quietly and hung up.

I stood there for a moment, surprised. Like most big sisters, I was a little on the bossy side. Sometimes I was impatient with Billy, and we squabbled. It wasn't like him not to take my bait. *Oh well*, I thought, shrugging, and went back to my game with Dad. A while later I was about to lay down my last card when Mom ran in. Immediately I knew something was wrong.

"Where's Billy?" she demanded breathlessly.

"He's at Johnny's. Why?"

"There was an accident by the school. A boy on a bike was killed by a car. I just drove past it." She lunged for the phone and dialed. I couldn't hear what she said, but I saw her face contort, turn white and then completely lose expression, all in the span of a few seconds. She dropped the receiver and cried in a strange, strangled voice, "It's Billy!"

The next few hours were chaotic. Friends and relatives streamed in and out of the house. Forgotten for a time, I slumped over the back of a chair, staring out the dining room window and seeing nothing. I had been trying to be brave in front of Mom and Dad; I knew they needed my help. But now they were in the kitchen, and I couldn't hold it in any longer. I laid my head in my arms and unleashed my grief in big, gulping sobs.

Lying in bed later all I could think about was how badly I had treated Billy. It wasn't the only time I had snapped at him. He must have thought I was his mean old sister, I concluded miserably. I wouldn't blame him if he didn't love me.

I didn't question God about why He had taken Billy. Mom was always telling us God had a good reason for everything, and I tried to believe that. But when Billy's quiet words kept bouncing off the insides of my head, "Bye, Debbie . . . Bye, Debbie," I couldn't help wondering why God hadn't allowed me the simple, small privilege of saying good-bye to him.

Restless, I rolled over. I felt something poking into my side. My stuffed dog. Angrily I picked it up and hurled it across the room. I heard the pop of one of its plastic eyes hitting the wall, and I fell back onto my pillow, tears about to overwhelm me again.

Suddenly I heard a man's gentle voice: "Don't worry about Billy. He's much happier here."

I sat up and called out softly, "Dad?"

There was no answer. Flinging back the covers, I went to the top of the stairs. I could hear a murmur from the kitchen. Looking down at the empty foyer, I began to wonder if I had imagined the voice.

Then I saw Mom at the bottom of the stairs, holding out her arms. How had she known I was there? I ran down the steps into her embrace and told her what I had heard. "I knew God would let us know that everything was all right," she said. "Thank you, Debbie."

God had comforted Mom, and for that I was grateful. But it didn't help my guilt. It was bad enough I hadn't shown my brother I loved him. Now I couldn't seem to remember what he looked like, how his voice sounded, or even the things we used to do together . . . it made me feel so cold, almost heartless.

God, forgive me for being mean to Billy, I prayed. *Please help me remember him*. But nothing came, not a single shred of memory.

Somehow I managed to get through the next weeks. It might have looked like I was back to enjoying my normal routine—school, chores, watching the kids—but I wasn't.

I was just going through the motions. It seemed as if a veil had dropped over my life, overshadowing everything so I couldn't really feel.

Two months after Billy's death, Mom insisted I take my bike to school to be inspected and registered. Since the accident, I hadn't wanted to ride my bike. It seemed disloyal to Billy to go on as if nothing had happened. I went, though, for Mom.

I ran the thirteen blocks to school, pushing my old blue bike and feeling savagely glad whenever a pedal struck my shin. *Billy should be doing this with me,* I thought. I watched resentfully as a police officer inspected and tagged my bike.

As I was leaving, I heard someone ask, "Aren't you Debbie Lupien?"

I turned and saw a girl a little younger than me. "Yes," I answered. "How did you know?"

She told me she was in Billy's class and I was just like he described me. "Actually, you look a lot like him," she added, "except for the curly hair and glasses."

"Billy talked about me?" I was astounded.

"He told us what a great dancer you are. And that you're the fastest typist in the whole school. He used to say, 'Even though my sister's the smallest girl in the sixth grade, she can do anything.'" She gave me a shy smile. "I'm sorry about the accident."

I was so stunned I didn't even thank her. I just stood

there, not caring that half the school could see the tears running down my face.

All at once, memories flooded my mind. I remembered sneaking into Billy's room at night to do jigsaw puzzles, teaching him how to punt a football, hitting flies and grounders to him. I remembered him sticking up for me when the other boys wouldn't let me play baseball because I was a girl. I could hear him declaring staunchly, "Deb's a better hitter than any of you." Most of all, I remembered how he would fling his head back, crunching up his eyes as he laughed at something I had said that wasn't funny to anyone but him.

Billy loved me, I thought incredulously. *He believed in me.* The veil that had fallen over everything in my life lifted. *Thank You, God, for giving back my memories of love.*

With a sudden burst of energy I ran with my bicycle across the grassy school yard. Turning toward home, I replayed Billy's words: *My big sister can do anything.* I could hear his laugh as I hopped on my bike and rode down the street, pumping the pedals faster and faster. Again I heard Billy say, "Bye, Debbie."

Finally I was able to answer, to speak the words inside my heart. "Good-bye, Billy," I whispered. The breeze brushed across my forehead, a gentle kiss from God.

Papaw's Crab Apple

by Jonnie Lauten Clemmons

I GREW UP WITH my two brothers and five sisters on a small farm in rural North Carolina. Our parents often seemed overwhelmed: They had too little time and money and too much laundry and cooking to deal with, not to mention the never-ending childhood illnesses and injuries.

Luckily they had help: our mother's parents, John and Bessie Yokley, whom we called Papaw and Mom. The two of them, my grandfather in particular, seemed as unshakable as the old crab apple that kept a solitary vigil in one of the fields. Papaw's father had planted it on the day Papaw was born, and the tree had survived drought, heat, floods and natural disasters in much the same stubborn fashion that my grandfather had weathered life's storms. I often climbed it when I needed to be alone to think.

I took it for granted Papaw would be around forever. That's why it came as such a shock when he became ill the winter after I turned sixteen, and instead of bouncing back as usual, he grew weaker and weaker.

As soon as it was warm enough, I climbed the crab apple and settled in a comfortable nook amid its thick, gnarled branches. My head wasn't filled with the thoughts that typically preoccupied me. I didn't think about who I was, what I would do when I grew up, or even about God. I thought about Papaw.

In my mind he wasn't the sickly old man his illness had made him, but the strong, barrel-chested force he had been all my life. Unruly white hair capped his lined, leathery face, and his blue eyes beamed alertly from behind his thick glasses. Clad in his standard uniform—Jack Rabbit overalls with patches on the knees and scuffed brogans with broken shoestrings—he worked tirelessly beside the eight of us grandchildren in the fields as we planted, picked, hoed and weeded. A lifelong farmer, Papaw loved and respected the land and its Creator.

Papaw was the backbone of our family and respected throughout the community. He was held in high esteem, as much for his knowledge of farming as for his honesty and integrity. My grandfather was also renowned for his intolerance of what he called slick talkers.

I smiled as I remembered the afternoon a salesman became acquainted with Papaw's biting wit.

That hot, dry summer day a dust-covered Volkswagen Beetle pulled into our driveway. A red-faced young man emerged, wearing a sweat-dampened seersucker suit. He dragged an unwieldy suitcase from the passenger seat and, putting on his most charming smile, headed for Papaw.

"Afternoon, Granddad. Hot one, huh?" My grandfather

didn't respond, but the young man was undeterred and proceeded to launch into a thirty-minute speech. When he was finished, the salesman paused expectantly. "Well, whaddya say, Granddad? Pretty impressive, huh?"

Shifting the piece of straw he had been chewing to the other side of his mouth, Papaw growled, "What in tarnation are you talking about?"

"Encyclopedias, sir," the young man said. "Books that tell you everything you want to know."

"Well, if anyone around here needs to know anything," my grandfather snorted, "they can come and ask me." Without another word, the salesman packed his books and slunk off.

I absently stroked the crab apple's smooth bark, lost in my reverie. But try as I might, I could not reconcile the tough, spirited presence of my memories with the frail man who had been too weak to take part in our springtime planting. I climbed down, feeling cheated out of the sense of comfort and security I usually gained from my perch in the crab apple.

Around the first of June, a severe thunderstorm struck. I had a bad feeling about Papaw's tree, and after the storm passed I went to check on it. The tree was still standing—but barely. Several limbs had been sheared off, and a crack cleaved the trunk almost in two. "He's going to die." The unwanted thought sprang from my lips before I was aware I had spoken.

The next day Papaw was taken to the hospital. He hung on for two weeks before a massive stroke ended his pain.

The afternoon of his funeral, another thunderstorm raged, toppling the crab apple. To me, Papaw and his tree had epitomized stability. My faith in the order of the world —and indeed, my faith in its Creator—was shaken to its very roots.

I couldn't talk about my sense of loss with anyone. Instead, I blamed God. He had betrayed my trust. He had taken my grandfather and left me to face life on my own. I lashed out at everyone who tried to comfort me. I took innumerable walks, trying to make sense of what had happened.

Always I found myself in the field, staring at the empty space where the crab apple had been. Sometimes I captured a fleeting sense of peace and acceptance. But eventually the thought of life without Papaw caused the deep, almost palpable ache of bitter loss to resurface.

Then one morning I awoke with the smoky remnants of a dream still drifting within my consciousness. I had dreamed I was walking and weeping, when I heard Papaw call my name. Amazed, I turned and saw him standing right where his tree had stood. Beside him was another person I didn't recognize. I ran up and for some reason knelt before them.

Tenderly chiding me for my tears, Papaw spoke of the happiness he had found in the place where he was now. He reminded me of the pain he had suffered during his life, especially his final days. The other figure stood back. I couldn't make out His features, but I sensed a radiance emanating from Him unlike anything I had ever witnessed.

"Jonnie, it's time for you to ask the Lord to forgive you for your anger and to heal your sorrow," Papaw said.

"But He's the one who killed you and left us all alone," I protested.

Papaw quoted from Psalm 1: "And he shall be like a tree planted by the rivers of water, that bringeth forth his fruit in his season; his leaf also shall not wither; and whatsoever he doeth shall prosper."

The other figure leaned over me and asked, "Do you suppose I would fail to watch over what I have so lovingly planted?"

Then both of them were gone.

What did my dream mean? I wasn't sure, but I knew where I had to go. I dressed quietly and slipped out of the bedroom I shared with my sisters. I headed to the familiar place in the field. When I finally stood at the spot, breathing in the fresh early-morning air, I felt oddly at peace. As in my dream, I suddenly knelt, ignoring the damp ground chilling my knees.

I looked down. There before me—incredibly—were eight small apple-tree shoots, their tender green tips pushing through the soil. They grew in twin clusters, with two shoots grouped on the left, and six grouped on the right.

Just like us grandchildren—two boys and six girls. God was looking out for us. Even without our beloved grandfather, the eight of us would be all right. God hadn't taken Papaw away, but had brought him closer into His embrace.

My tears fell, dotting the earth where the crab apple had once stood. But this time they were the healthy, healing tears of acceptance and gratitude and love—for Papaw and for God.

PART VIII

Direction for Life

Oh, send out Your light and Your truth!
Let them lead me;
Let them bring me to Your holy hill
And to Your tabernacle.

Psalm 43:2–3 NKJV

SOMETIMES THE HEAVENLY COMFORT sent to us serves to direct our actions, setting us on a godly path or even guiding career choices. One morning after widowed Carol Oden had turned to tranquilizers to deal with her "regrets and despair," she pointedly asked Jesus what she should do. The immediate answer amazed her: "Wash the dishes." For Carol, one positive decision led to others, until her life stabilized. Dixon Hill and Patrick Middleton have internalized mottos learned from soldiers—a colleague and a father —who passed away, leaving this valued legacy. Several stories in this section are even more dramatic: angels and visions, light received, direction accepted, lives changed.

The Sergeant's Boots

by Dixon Hill

ORT BRAGG, NORTH CAROLINA, summer of 1988. I was a sergeant and one of five hundred soldiers signed up for one of the Army's toughest tests: a six-month-long Special Forces Qualification Course to become a Green Beret. Most of the guys were infantrymen—macho, football-player types, with the kind of build you see on the cover of a fitness magazine. They were used to hoofing for miles with heavy field packs. I was chunky and out of shape. My background was military intelligence, where I basically sat at a desk all day and analyzed information. In high school, I was first string—on the chess team, if that helps you get the picture.

I wasn't surprised when no one would give me the time of day. Why bother with someone who had "washout" written all over him?

So I was startled when Sergeant John Hall came up to me the day after the grueling land navigation test, a sort of preview of what lay ahead. Each of us had to hike alone in the dead of night in full gear, through miles of rough hills and swampland, without the benefit of trails or even a flashlight, and finish just after dawn. John had been one of the first finishers. Naturally, I'd been practically last. I was still exhausted from the ordeal.

"My name's John," he said, sticking out his hand. John looked to be in his early twenties. He had a down-hollow accent; later I'd learn he was from deep in the hills of West Virginia. A trainee like me, he was the most gung ho soldier in our outfit. His uniform fit like a custom suit, and his black, standard-issue combat boots were buffed like a new pair of dress shoes. I could tell he felt pity for me and I wanted none of it.

"I'm Dixon Hill," I said. "You don't have to talk to me. I understand why guys are ignoring me."

I figured it was pointless to try to change people's minds about me. But I knew the truth. I bled army green. As a kid, I loved listening to my dad's stories about serving as an Army engineer in the Philippines after World War II. I joined the Arizona National Guard at eighteen. I had always dreamed of being a Green Beret.

Of course, John didn't know all that. But I relaxed a little when he smiled and said, "You'll be here tomorrow, and the day after, and the day after that until you graduate. You got it in you; I can tell. Just keep doing the right thing."

Training school was even tougher than advertised. And there was more to it than just physical strength. One day I had to make camp in the woods and then kill and cook a caged animal that would feed me for two days. I chose rabbit. I attempted to roast it with little success. "You should have picked a chicken," John told me. "And you should have boiled it—boiling's faster. I learned that from my daddy when we went hunting." He hiked back to his campsite and brought me some of his meal. I was chagrined but grateful.

People dropped out left and right. Some failed the field tests, others collapsed from physical strain and some flat-out quit. At the halfway point, just 175 of us remained. One day, after parachuting into a drop zone, one of the football types eyed me and snorted, "Hill, you're still here?"

I was, barely. I still wasn't in very good shape. During one brutal full-gear hike through the North Carolina hills, I slumped against a tree. I wanted to sleep for a solid week. John sat down. "How you doing?" he asked.

"This is the hardest thing I've ever done," I said. "I'm not sure I can make it."

John looked at me, and then he did something funny. He bent down and patted his shiny combat boots. "We all use little tricks to keep us going," he said. "Mine are these boots. They ain't made for standing still. They're God's reminder to me to keep moving when times are tough. You need to just keep doing the next right thing."

Pretty soon I felt myself getting stronger. I looked forward to physical tests. Guys began to eat with me and shoot the breeze. Slowly but surely, I sensed that I was being accepted and that I belonged.

Now that I could keep up, I ran with John in drills. One of our last was the rucksack run test: a torturous fifteen-mile sprint through hill country wearing heavy backpacks. We had three and a half hours to finish. John ran directly in front of me. All day I passed guys who'd collapsed in their tracks. But you were supposed to keep running, no matter what.

I cleared the last rise. The finish line was fifteen yards ahead. "Made it!" I started to say. Then suddenly, John went down like he'd been shot. *I have to stop. I have to help him up.* But then I remembered our orders. I jumped over John and completed the race.

It was only then that I looked back. John was still lying there. A medic raced down the path. I prayed as the medic administered CPR. *Come on, big guy.*

John didn't revive. He was dead of a massive heart attack.

My grief turned to guilt. The bottoms of my boots were probably the last things John had seen. I should have stopped.

The Army flew John's body home to his family in West Virginia. Our unit held its own memorial service. I marched into Fort Bragg's Special Warfare Center chapel, my mind spinning. If I had stopped to help, could I have saved him? The medic told me no. Still, I couldn't forgive myself.

The pastor put John's boots—spit-shined to a mirror

finish—on the chapel altar. An M16 rifle stood upside down between them. A green beret rested on top of the rifle. The army had awarded it to John posthumously. *Lord, I prayed, I can't live with the possibility that I didn't do the right thing.*

The pastor spoke movingly, but my mind drifted. I thought about that time John shared his boiled chicken with me.

The company commander rose. We stood at attention as the captain called roll. "Here, sir!" soldiers barked back, as we went down the line. Then the captain shouted, "John Hall!"

Silence.

The captain paused, then continued. "Dixon Hill!"

"Here, sir!"

On it went until the last name was called. Again the captain said, "Is Sergeant John Hall of West Virginia here?"

Once more, silence.

His voice wavering, the captain shouted, "Last call! Sergeant John Hall!" I stood ramrod straight, trying to ignore the stinging in my eyes. *My friend is gone. Do I have the strength to go on?*

Just then a flash of light came. Brilliant light. The light reflected from John's boots on the altar. It was so bright I couldn't tear my eyes away. The effect made the boots glow, and its glow engulfed me. I heard John say again,

"God had the Army issue us these boots to keep us moving, even when times are tough."

Years have passed since that day at the base chapel. I'm out of the Army now, retired from the Green Berets. I'm forty years old and in college, studying for a new career. Sometimes, in the middle of a tough assignment, I think of John. The other day, I dug my old Army boots out of the closet. I can't wear them anymore; they're faded and cracked, and the leather is splitting. But they are there to remind me: Yes, times can get tough. But the tough get through tough times. They just do the next right thing.

Next to Godliness

by Carol Oden

I DON'T SUPPOSE there is any good way to prepare for the death of a loved one. But when my husband died, leaving me and our six children, I was devastated. At night I lay wide-eyed with grief and panic, wondering how I would provide for my kids, especially my three teenagers, who needed a strong, guiding hand. During the day I dragged around the house, exhausted by regrets and despair. The children mirrored my moods with angry outbursts; our home was an unhappy place.

When my doctor advised me to take a vacation, I laughed bitterly and settled for his second-best suggestion: a regimen of tranquilizers. The boys called them "Mom's downers." It terrified me that they knew this term. Drugs were rampant at their high school. A neighbor boy who had grown up with the kids was found dead from an overdose in his car on Main Street, and another had died driving drunk after a party. Would my children consider my dependence on tranquilizers a green light to drug experimentation?

One dismal morning after yet another sleepless night, I stood alone in my cluttered kitchen, too weary and confused to do anything but stare out the window. I closed my eyes and pleaded, *Jesus, if You were standing here beside me, what would You tell me to do?*

Immediately I heard: *Wash the dishes.*

I was startled . . . and disappointed. I had expected, if anything, something more profound. But when I opened my eyes, all I could see before me were messy dishes. I filled the sink with hot, soapy water. This one square foot of cleanliness gave the kitchen a curious lightness. In my fatigue, I could only cope with one dish at a time. Yet soon the task was over, the dishes in the cupboard. I cleared away the accumulation of odds and ends that cluttered the counters. The kitchen looked much better. Now what?

Sweep, then mop the floor.

I did, and I waxed it for good measure. Now the entire kitchen glowed. It smelled fresh and clean. For the first time in months, I took a deep breath.

Energized, I went from room to room, keeping up my dialogue with the Lord. By the time the children returned from school, the house was neat and clean. I had a batch of cookies, still warm from the oven, ready for them. A pot of soup simmered on the stove. I had worked like a fiend, but when the kids said, "Wow, Mom, great cookies!" I felt as if I had just woken from a nap.

That day was the beginning of our new life. If I started to yell at a child, I stopped. It had become clear that harsh words had no place in a clean, orderly household. In a tranquil house, tranquilizers were no longer necessary. Calmly I discussed drugs with the kids, and together, we escaped their scourge. I telephoned creditors, asking them to help me work out payment schedules I could handle.

Nothing about the basics of our situation changed. There never was enough money. I still struggled to put food on the table for six hungry kids, and I still grieved the loss of my husband. Yet after I had obeyed a simple command, our house turned into a place where our family could restore itself.

Then everything changed.

Whistlin' Willie

by Patrick Middleton

OULD I EVER EXPLAIN how lost and alone I felt sitting at the desk in his den, his books and papers scattered around me, his photographs up on the wall? My father had just died. And I found myself in that old chair of his, half expecting him to come into the room at any moment and catch me there. If only he could talk me through my grief and help me find my way.

Above me hung models of every plane he ever flew, suspended from the ceiling on thin black thread. And there he was, up on the wall in all his glory—his life shown in the pictures carefully displayed on a backdrop of dark paneling. My father as a young man in his leather flight jacket, a silver plane behind him. That wonderful, boyish smile of his was repeated in almost every snapshot, from his World War II days to his days at Cape Kennedy. Looking at my father's smile, seeing him young and strong again, I couldn't bring myself to believe that this man, Stan Middleton, was gone.

He had been a pilot in World War II, splitting his time between tours of combat in Europe and stints stateside, where he helped develop techniques to fly big B-17 bombers north to Alaska without having them ice up. After the war, he worked on jet engines for General Electric and then got a job at NASA to help with the Apollo launches. Sitting at his desk, I felt incredibly proud of my father. I had a wonderful wife and family and a career as a counselor, all of which gave me great satisfaction. But I never accomplished anything like he had. The war, the space program—he'd been a leader in a heroic generation of Americans.

I leafed through his clippings and papers, absently fingering the wooden arm of his chair, trying to piece together the things he told me those last couple of days. He had gone so quickly, in less than a week. I had been at his bedside, rubbing his cold hands, Dad slipping in and out of consciousness. We shared long spells of silence, but he also told me things about his life, things he'd never told me before. He was surprised by how fast the years had gone by. "Almost eighty years, Pat, and it's gone just like that," he said.

He lay there listless much of the time. Then he'd turn onto his side, fully awake, asking to have more ice or water. He'd cough and take a sip and appear like a man who would live another twenty years. The next moment, he looked like a man who'd just taken his final breath. At one point, in the small hours of the night, my father suddenly sat up on his elbows. He wanted to tell me a story, he said, the story of Whistlin' Willie. So I propped him up with some pillows, and he talked while I listened.

In the war, he had made long bombing runs over Germany. More than once, he told me that night, the pilots had flown back to England only to find their airfield outside London fogged in. With wounded airmen onboard and dangerously low on fuel, the formation would limp on to the next base. Some men died en route. And some damaged planes never made it. It seemed an extravagant waste, the planes and men surviving bombing runs only to be lost to the English fog.

This didn't sit well with Captain Middleton. In his spare time, he and a flight engineer worked on a battle-damaged B-17. It kept them busy during the long days when they didn't fly, rebuilding the ramshackle aircraft, part by part, piece by piece. One part they couldn't replace was the propeller on one of the engines. The prop had been hit with a .50-caliber shell. It made an incredible wail as wind streamed through the hole when the engines cranked up. "It was absolutely piercing," Dad said, "just about the loudest thing I'd ever heard." But it could still fly. Hearing the plane taxi down the runway one day, someone in the control tower dubbed it "Whistlin' Willie." The name stuck.

Whistlin' Willie would never be combat-ready, but my dad convinced the control tower to let him test-fly it over the base. It must have been then, circling the base on that ribbon of sound, that the idea came to him. Could he lead those other planes through the fog with this one?

My father went to the navigation specialists: Was there

a way to rig up some device on the old plane to locate the runway through the fog? He went to the radio technicians: Could he fix on a radio signal and use a locator, compass, clock and altimeter to plot a flight path? Only after he had everything lined up did my father approach the commanding officer for the go-ahead.

The morning was foggy when word arrived that a squadron of planes was returning to base. They'd sustained heavy fire and there were wounded.

The CO volunteered to hold a radio microphone button down for a constant signal. Radar was in its infancy, and this was how Dad might find the base through the worst weather conditions. The call was sent out to the approaching fliers: "Look for Whistlin' Willie," the base radioman told them. "He's gonna lead you home through the fog."

Not knowing what this meant, the pilots searched the sky. They were ragged, tired and afraid of the fog, thick as soup below them. But Captain Middleton put on his flight suit and throttled that old B-17 screaming down the runway. The old barn of a plane took flight, circling over the signal of the radio microphone, the windshield streaked and wet with the clouds Dad was flying through. The sound of the engines and propellers thundered so loud he could feel them in his chest as he turned and turned, constantly checking the clock, the signal locator and the altimeter in the widening circle over the airbase.

The first glimpse of sun broke across his wings as he

breached the surface of clouds. Then he was circling over a floor of gray cotton, London hidden from view, the B-17 rattling as if ready to fall apart at the seams. And there, in the distance, he caught the glint of light from the other planes approaching.

The returning planes fell into formation behind him, those that were either damaged or carrying wounded moving into line first. He could take only a few planes at a time, so he led the first string down through the fog, the pilots all trusting the lead of Captain Middleton and Whistlin' Willie.

The pilots had to depend on one another to provide visual confirmation that they were taking the right flight path through the fog, the followers becoming leaders for those behind them. And if a pilot was spooked by the fog and couldn't see, the control tower told him to lean out the window and listen carefully for the screaming propeller up ahead; the sound would help guide him safely to the airstrip.

Dad led the way until the airfield could be seen. Fifty yards from the tarmac, he pulled up and buzzed the control tower. Then he banked the plane back into the fog, circling up for the next set of planes.

"I can't tell you how many planes we guided down through the fog in those last months of the war," my father said. "But it was the best thing I've ever done in my life." He fell silent and closed his eyes after that, his cheeks more hollow than I remembered, his breaths shallow and growing quiet as he fell asleep. It was the last story my father told me. After that it was mostly ice chips, cool washcloths and squeezes of his hand until he passed, early in the morning.

After his death, the image of that plane holding a string of souls by a thread of sound—its whistle in the dark— kept coming back to me. I wondered what my father meant by this story. But I had to deal with mundane matters such as his will, his insurance policy, his bank accounts. Besides, there was the raw grief.

Now, as I sat quiet at his desk, though, staring at the photos on the wall, my father seemed to smile down at me with that same boyish grin of his. *Trust*, it said. *You may be lost in a fog of grief now, but you'll make it through. You'll find your way home.*

How? I wondered staring at the photos, and remembering that last war story.

The answer came suddenly. *Follow the lead of others*, I could almost hear him say. *There will be people to help you: your minister, lawyer, counselor, friends, wife, children. When you can't see the way, God will give you people to guide you. Listen for them. That is how God will lead you.*

At last the fog was clearing.

The House Where Mom's Love Lived

by LaVonne "Voni" Potter

SLOWLY I DROVE THROUGH my hometown of Hazel Park, Michigan, just north of Detroit, my older sister, Vivian, beside me. "Everything looks so different," I said, as we passed the site of my junior high school, where now a Holiday Inn stood. A little farther, the soccer field I used to play on had been converted into a parking lot.

I hadn't been back for twenty years, not since my mother and father had both passed away. Vivian's husband had recently passed on too, so I'd come to stay with her for a while in Madison Heights, northeast of Detroit. We decided to drive around Hazel Park one afternoon and reminisce.

We stopped at Oakview Cemetery and laid flowers on Mom's grave. As we got back in the car, my mind filled with memories. Mom had been a minister and taught Sunday school for many years in this area.

"I can't count how many missionaries passing through came to have Sunday dinner with us," I said to Vivian. "Even though Mom didn't like cooking much, she never turned anyone away."

"I can still hear her singing hymns and playing the piano," Vivian said. "She had such a nice voice."

Our mother often took in friends and neighbors in need. One time an invalid woman whose husband was an alcoholic stayed for weeks. I heard my mother late at night, listening to her, counseling her.

"But you don't even know her," I said to Mom one afternoon. "Why do you do so much for her?"

"LaVonne, each of us only stays on this earth a short time, but the good we do for others never goes away. The greatest joy in this life is helping someone who needs it."

If a neighbor's child fell out of a tree or off his bike, it was always Mom who volunteered to take him to the hospital. If someone was sick, Mom was the one who sat by her bedside and read to her from the Bible.

Once, a young woman whose husband had lost his job started attending our church. Shortly after, her husband committed suicide. When Mom heard, she turned to me. "Put on a jacket, LaVonne, we're driving over there." I was scared to go to a house with so much sadness, but Mom reassured me. "There is no one so unhappy you can't comfort her," she said, "no one so low that another human being reaching out to her can't raise her up."

I went with Mom night after night as she comforted that young woman. Mom even delivered the eulogy at the husband's funeral.

Now I looked out the car window at Mom's church as

Vivian and I drove by. It looked large and unfamiliar. The whole town was so much bigger and more crowded. We passed family-owned restaurants we used to eat in while I was growing up, but the names on the signs were different —not the families we knew. Little neighborhood shops had become supermarkets and discount stores. As we rounded a corner, I knew we were getting close to our old house. Dad had built the two-bedroom bungalow with the help of some friends when I was seven. I remembered how he'd push me back and forth on the swing he'd set up in the yard, how Mom would wave to me from the kitchen window.

"Let's stop by and see if they'll let us look around," I suggested to Vivian. She nodded, and I parked on the street. We walked to the door. Our white picket fence was gone, as well as the big oak tree out front. I guess nothing lasts forever. I rang the doorbell, and it was answered by a young woman holding a little girl.

"Sorry to bother you," I said, "but my father built this house, and we were wondering if we might come inside for a moment."

"Oh," the woman said, looking over her shoulder at her husband, who was sitting on the couch watching television. "Honey, we have visitors," she said. "They used to live here." He looked up at us. "Come on in," he said.

Vivian and I introduced ourselves. As the young woman got us something to drink, her husband showed us around.

Again, I was shocked by how many things had changed. The layout of the kitchen was different, as well as the windows and the carpeting. We stepped out back, and I saw that the swing set and plaster playhouse Dad had built for me were gone. Back inside, we sat on the couch and sipped our drinks. It was cozy and warm, and I was very comfortable talking with the young family. Still, I felt a pang of loss as I searched for some mark left by my parents, some remnant of the years they had lived in this house. *You'd never even know they were once here*, I thought sadly.

I thought of all the memories I had made within these walls. Not just as a child, but later, as an adult, a wife and mother who introduced a new generation to the love that lived here. "When my son Donald was born, I brought him straight from the hospital to this house," I said. "Later, on visits, he used to spend whole afternoons on the swing that used to be out back. Then he'd run inside to get a green apple from the little box Mom and Dad kept in the cupboard just for him."

I noticed a Bible lying on the end table and thought of Mom's well-worn holy book, always close at hand. I told the young couple how Mom had pastored several churches and about all the people she'd helped and encouraged over the years.

The young woman's eyes widened. "Your mom was that kind of a person?" she said. "I guess that explains it."

"Explains what?" I asked.

She glanced at her husband, and he nodded his head as if she had something important to say. "Tell them," he said.

"Well, when we moved into this house, we weren't in very good shape," she said. "I'd started using drugs, and they took over my life. I couldn't stop, not even after our child was born. Sometimes late at night when I was lying awake, I'd sense this force directing me to read my Bible. It was a real gentle presence, almost like my own mama trying to nudge me back on the right track."

The young woman picked up the Bible from the end table and thumbed through the pages. "There were so many nights when the words in here were the only thing keeping me going," she said. "But then one night I was at the end of my rope. My family was falling apart. I didn't see any way out except to end it all. And I didn't want to leave my baby behind, so I was going to take her with me." The woman paused and took her husband's hand. She gazed around the living room. The little girl sat on the floor, doing a puzzle.

"And then I felt that presence," the woman went on. "I'd never felt such a loving force in my whole life. It seemed to fill up this entire room. I knew it was telling me not to go through with what I was planning, but I didn't want to listen. I didn't want any more pain. Still, the force held strong. It was telling me to raise up my hands and ask God for His help. Finally I sank down onto my knees and did just that. That's the day my life began again."

I looked around the room, and this time every unfamiliar object seemed suddenly dear to me, touched by Mom's spirit. It was like she was right there with us, humming hymns and making beds for our guests. Yes, I was sure that the presence that had saved the young family was a manifestation of God's love, the same love that had been the core of Mom's life.

We thanked the young couple and wished them well. At the doorway, I looked back into the house one last time, the house that had changed so much over the years. Mom's love inhabited this house, just as her spirit lived on in me each time I reached out to help someone. Like Mom said, the good we do lives on. That will never change.

PART IX

Gifts from God

The people asked, and He brought quail,
And satisfied them with the bread of heaven.
He opened the rock and water gushed out;
It ran in the dry places like a river.

Psalm 105:40–41 NKJV

"NOW I KNEW WHAT IT WAS LIKE to drink fully of God's grace," says widow Frieda Sheen. She's describing a gift of God sent in an hour of trial: a new appreciation for home and friends.

Gifts and gratitude. The words belong together, even for men and women living with the painful realities of loss.

Life itself—time—can be viewed as a gift. But the writers featured in this section describe specific experiences— many would be described as miracles—in which God bestows His grace. A salvaged marriage and spiritual awakening after the death of a son. A special hand-crafted bird. Turn the page and discover a gift in printed words: Anne Sternad's moving story of her son T.J. and what he left behind after his untimely death.

The Unopened Gift

by Anne Sternad

IT WAS SUCH AN UNUSUAL THING for T.J. to say.

We were walking in the snow outside our house that cold November afternoon when I reached down, hugged my five-year-old son and told him how much I loved him. Terry Junior looked up through his beautiful green blue eyes and said, "I love you too, Mommy, more than anything in the world—except God. I love Him a little bit more!"

I laughed and tousled his sandy hair. "Well," I said, "as long as it's God, that's okay."

Where in the world has he heard about God? I wondered. God was never mentioned in our house. I had not thought much about God for years, and my husband Terry was practically an atheist. Neither of us felt we had need of anything spiritual in our lives. Young and successful, we were doing quite well on our own. We lived in Denver, where Terry was a corporate executive, and I was busy raising our two children.

But T.J.'s declaration of love wasn't the only strange thing that happened in those days. For a week he had been trying to give me his Christmas gift, which he had bought at a "Secret Santa Shop." Each time he offered me the little box, wrapped in colored paper, I would laugh. "Honey, it's too early! Please put it away." Finally I took it and said we'd keep it safe in my closet until Christmas.

That night I told Terry about the unopened gift, and I mentioned T.J.'s words about God. "Could they have had something to do with the death of your mother six months ago?" I asked. Both T.J. and his eight-year-old sister Samantha had wondered where she had gone. To soothe them I had said, "With God, in heaven."

Terry nodded thoughtfully.

"And remember," I continued, "not long after that, you and I were talking at the dinner table in front of the children about the man in your office—the one who keeps talking to you about God and Jesus?"

"Yes," he said, "Don, who always asks me to think about where I'll spend eternity. He just doesn't give up."

But we were never to know for sure what caused T.J. to speak as he did. In fact, that night my talk with Terry flared into an argument about other matters. Truth was, our marriage was in trouble. We had grown apart through the years. Now we often found fault, bickered and snapped at each other. If it hadn't been for Samantha and T.J., we would have parted long ago.

The children remained my greatest solace. I especially doted on T.J. Only recently I had told a friend just how I felt about him. "If anything ever happens to that little guy,"

I said, "you can lock me up and throw away the key, because I don't know how I would get through it."

I found out that terrible gray December day.

My parents had come for a holiday visit, and we all had gone to a stable on the outskirts of Denver, where Samantha was learning to ride. We planned to take pictures of the children astride a horse for our family Christmas card. It was so cold that Samantha rode her horse inside, up and down the shed row between the stalls. As usual, T.J. ran about making friends with everyone, from stable workers to visitors. When Samantha was through with her lesson, I said, "Go get your brother so we can take the Christmas picture."

She came back in a few minutes: "I can't find T.J. anywhere." A chill clutched me. Terry hurried away to look, and I ran to my parents. They hadn't seen T.J. either. I thought of the frozen creek that meandered near the stables. Outside, scanning the flat snow-covered land, I could see no one. I called for T.J., but there was only eerie silence. Meanwhile, my parents and Terry questioned everyone in the area, even canvassing homes that bordered the stable property. My calls had turned to screams, and I was stumbling through the snow when Terry came up and took my arm.

"We've looked everywhere," he said huskily. "I'm calling the police."

I fell to my knees in the snow, crying, pleading. "Oh,

God, I'll go to church every week. I'll put our children in Sunday school," I bargained. "I'll do anything if You'll please bring my baby back!"

Terry led me with Samantha to a nearby house where a woman gave me a tranquilizer. I huddled under a quilt, rocking back and forth, crying for my little boy. Hours passed. At around two in the afternoon, the people who were trying to comfort me suddenly became quiet. I looked up and saw Terry's grief-stricken face. He knelt and put his arm around me.

"They found him," he said quietly. I didn't want to hear the details of how T.J. had wandered onto a snow-covered pond and had fallen through the ice. "The doctors said he didn't suffer, Anne," said Terry. "The water was so cold he lost consciousness instantly."

The room seemed to fade away for a moment. I remember Terry telling me they were taking T.J. to the hospital, where doctors thought there was a one-in-a-million chance to revive him. More hours seemed to pass as I waited for word. Then there was a call from the hospital: A heartbeat had been found. Hope glimmered. I sat up and, dabbing tear stains from my face, got out my makeup. "T.J. always told me I was beautiful," I said. "I don't want him to see me like this." But there was to be one more call from the hospital. Terry came over and said, "He's gone."

When we walked into our house, now so deadly quiet, the terrible impact of losing T.J. hit me even worse than before. I stood transfixed in the hallway. I wanted to scream, but I couldn't. I stared blindly, my chest convulsing with short gasps. Terry raced upstairs and closed the door to T.J.'s room. I felt myself reeling on the edge of madness.

That's when a picture flashed before me: the gift T.J. had tried so often to give me. I dashed upstairs to our room and reached up to the closet shelf. My fingers touched the package. Pulling it down, I quickly tore away the paper. There in my hand lay a little gold-colored cross on a chain.

As it wavered in my blurred vision and my hand closed tightly on it, I knew with definite certainty where T.J. was—with Jesus Christ in heaven. T.J.'s little cross had broken through that hard, icy wall surrounding me, and I felt myself standing in His presence.

The serenity that flooded into me at that moment must have been visible. Terry stepped over and asked me if I was all right.

I took his hand. "I'm okay, Terry," I whispered. When I showed him T.J.'s gift, he hugged me in silence and wept.

After the funeral, Terry and I did not speak of T.J. We were so numbed, so preoccupied with our own feelings that we barely spoke at all. The snarling and bickering had stopped, but we seemed to live completely separate lives.

One day I looked up addresses of several Christian bookstores. I drove to all of them, and in each one I searched for books that would tell me more about Jesus and heaven. It was like when your child goes off on a trip to another country and you want to find out everything you can about that place. I found myself desperately wanting to know how to get there myself.

The next surprise came a month later. The front bell rang, and when I opened the door, a middle-aged, casually dressed stranger smiled at me. "Hello," he said, "I'm Terry's pastor."

I stepped back in complete shock. Terry was away, but I invited Rev. Luther Larson into our living room and listened in amazement as he said how pleased he was to have a new member of his congregation. Then we talked about T.J. He spoke of a couple at his church who had lost a baby daughter to meningitis.

"You could help one another," he said. As he left, he added that he hoped to see me at his service.

That night the separate paths Terry and I had been traveling came together. During a long talk, Terry told me his story. "Remember Don—the man who kept trying to talk to me about God?" he said. "Well, on that terrible afternoon while T.J. was in the hospital, I called Don for prayer. He put me in touch with Pastor Larson, and I've gone to his church several times since then." He looked up: "Would you ever think of going with me?"

My voice caught. "Oh, Terry," I cried, "yes!" And I told him of my journeys to the bookstores.

Terry and I went to that church and met the parents who had lost their baby. Our visits led to a deep friendship. This was the first of many encounters with bereaved mothers and fathers, who have become our special mission. We believe that any solace we have offered in their time of sorrow is still another part of the gift T.J. gave us.

The True View

by Frieda Sheen

ALLING MY BLACK LAB into the bathroom for his bath, I pushed the door shut behind us to keep the hall carpet dry. "Good boy," I said as I lathered Brutus up. As always, he was a good boy during his bath. I rinsed him off. Then he shook himself, spattering water over the entire room, which wasn't saying much. The spare bathroom in my mobile home was no bigger than a closet. There's just the tub, basin and toilet. Not even a window.

I toweled Brutus off and blotted my slacks where they had gotten wet. Brutus licked his graying muzzle and looked expectantly at the door. It was a lovely July day and both of us were eager to be outside. "I agree with you, Brutus. Let's get out of here," I said.

I twisted the doorknob and pulled. It didn't open.

I pulled again, harder. The door was stuck fast. Grabbing the knob in both hands, I tugged and tugged. I pounded the steel frame and jerked at the door again. Nothing. "What are we going to do, boy?" He sat down, looking at me as if I should know the answer.

I glanced at my watch: 10:30. It was a Thursday morning. How long till anyone missed me or even thought about me? My whole reason for moving to this community had been to be self-sufficient. People at church wouldn't inquire after me until Sunday. I hadn't wanted to be the kind of widow who was always calling on others for help, and I hadn't made a lot of friends here since I moved. I sat down on the lid of the toilet and scratched Brutus' ears.

"Of course," I told him, "there are the Carters. They'll check up on us." The Carters lived just thirty feet away in the next mobile home and looked in on me every now and then. Joanne even cut my grass most Saturday mornings.

I tried the door again—nothing happened—and then checked my watch. Seven minutes. It felt like seven hours. Brutus regarded me with doleful eyes. Maybe I can use his collar on the door. I took it off and tried forcing the buckle between the doorframe and lock. No good. The phone rang. Probably someone trying to sell me something. Who else called on a weekday morning? Not my kids. The five of them were busy with their own lives.

The bathroom was so small that Brutus and I kept bumping into each other. I stood, then sat, then stood. I heard a scratching. My cat! "Hello, Kramer," I called. His paw shot through the two-inch crack under the door. "Are you hungry, Kramer?" Maybe he'd get so hungry he'd alert a neighbor. Then I remembered his demand feeder. Kramer could get his food by himself. He could go for days on his own. Just like me: Not much of a bother.

I stared at the wall just a foot from my face. How narrow my life had become! I'd remarried after my divorce, and we'd moved to a spacious apartment. But when my second husband died, I moved to this mobile home community. No big garden to weed or house to clean. I told myself I didn't need much to be happy: Brutus, Kramer, our home. Wasn't that enough?

That's when the first one appeared. I wouldn't call it a vision exactly. There wasn't anything scary about it, more like a movie. One moment I was staring at a bathroom wall. The next, I could see an unlimited vista: a beautiful valley dotted with evergreen trees that grew before my eyes. It was as though God was saying to me, *I give you space. Even in this claustrophobic room.* It gave me peace all afternoon, until it faded.

At five the phone rang again. I listened to the ring echo in the empty mobile home. Loneliness swept back over me. My husband gone. My four sons and their families living more than a thousand miles away. My daughter was nearer, but her job kept her on the road for days. There were so few people in my life. At church I would hang back when introductions were made. Who'd want to bother with a seventy-two-year-old widow?

Then, amazingly, another picture appeared, right where

I was staring. I saw people, scores of them. They were walking toward me. No one I recognized, but all seemed like potential friends. The picture lasted only a minute but left an indelible message: *I give you friends*. It was a clear message, as sure as a ringing phone. God didn't mean for me to live in some self-imposed isolation.

I cupped my hands under the faucet and drank. Neither of us had eaten anything since breakfast, but we could drink. "Have some water, Brutus," I said, turning on the tub faucet. He refused. It was as if he knew he could not get outdoors and didn't want to wet the floor.

Eight o'clock; dark soon. I tried the door again. No luck. I unscrewed one lightbulb for a reserve and turned off the other light. I sat on the toilet lid, facing the wall, my head in my hands, dozing. I kept checking my glowing watch. Ten o'clock, midnight, three o'clock.

Sunup. I listened for noise in the street. People going to work. Every time a car passed, I banged on the walls with my fists and kicked at the door. "Speak, Brutus!" I said. If only he weren't such a gentleman. But no, he would never bark in such a confined space.

How could I last another minute, let alone another day? I thought of how careful I had been, finding this affordable place to live. I never wanted to become a burden to my children. As my mood began to nosedive again, I felt the urge to look at the wall. Another picture. I saw a huge wooden paddle like the ones used to cook pizza. A large hand was holding it. *God's hand*, I thought. The paddle was covered with little loaves of bread. I could hear God: *I will provide for you*. For the rest of the day, I kept thinking of that blessed abundance. Strangely enough, it satisfied my hunger.

Friday night. My watch said it was ten o'clock. We'd been in this bathroom thirty-six hours. Brutus backed into one corner and wet the floor for the first time. He looked mortified. "Poor old friend," I said. "That's all right." I worried that he was suffering from dehydration. Still, he wouldn't drink. I stared at the wall. One last picture came to me. A golden city, shimmering in the sunlight.

A bleak little room—what was so luxurious about that? Now I knew. God was present, and wherever He appeared, splendor followed. I gave up all my worries. I completely let go. I felt my whole body, my whole being, let go. Brutus and I would be rescued. God would see to it. Until then, His presence was everywhere. I had nothing to fear.

Saturday morning I turned the light on. I listened to the sounds outside of a lazy summer Saturday. People mowing their lawns and cutting their hedges. People walking their dogs. Suddenly I heard the tool-shed door creak open. Joanne had come over to mow my lawn. I jumped up and shouted and pounded on the walls until I heard the mower start. The moment the mower shut down, I screamed until I was hoarse.

At last I heard the doorbell ring. Joanne had come back with her husband Gary. "Are you okay, Frieda?" he called.

"No. I'm locked in the bathroom!"

"I'll get a locksmith." Half an hour later, I heard their voices and a second man's, and then someone fiddling with the front door. In moments the locksmith was at the bathroom door. Brutus' tail whipped back and forth. There was a pop and the door flew open. I gave Joanne a huge hug. Brutus' whole rear end wagged. Kramer crept out of his hiding place and took a playful swat at Brutus. I filled his water bowl to the brim, and he drank and drank.

I had been thirsty, too, in the bathroom, thirsty for assurance of God's presence. Now I knew what it was like to drink fully of God's grace.

Next Sunday the pastor asked if anyone had any stories about what God had been doing in their lives. I sprang to my feet and told about my ordeal and what I'd seen on the walls. I wanted people to know that though I was trapped, I did not feel trapped. And I see my life differently today than I did before.

Every chance I get, I tell people that when we try too hard to be self-sufficient, we are not only hurting ourselves but we are also robbing others of the chance to help us. That is not part of God's plan. You can never feel poor or alone when you are willing to let people into your life. That was the true view from the tiny bathroom in my mobile home.

A Golden Gift

by Patricia Lorenz

I NEVER KNEW WHETHER TO PAY any attention to those voices that pop into my head every once in a while, until I met Art, "The Swami of Origami," so proclaimed on his business card. A friend had told me that Art was a professional chair caner, and I had an old rocking chair that needed a new cane seat. So when my friend gave me Art's business card, I was surprised to learn that he was also a creative paper folder.

When I arrived at his house with my rocker, I discovered a man of many talents. Not only was Art a children's librarian at a large branch of the Milwaukee Public Library, but he was also a professional storyteller and a children's hospital chaplain. His hobby, origami, was evident all over the house. Delicate and intricate birds, beasts, boxes, houses and ribbons of brightly colored folded paper were on display everywhere, forming borders along the ceilings in every room.

We talked about Art's paper folding and his job as chaplain at the hospital. We talked about life and people. I learned quickly that Art was a man of great feeling and zest for life. After making arrangements to pick up my chair in a week, Art walked me to the door.

"Do you mind if I ask you a question?" he asked slowly.

"Not at all," I responded. Somehow I knew he was about to ask something important.

"Have you ever heard a little voice inside your head telling you to do something you didn't understand?"

"Well, I suppose so," I said slowly, not sure exactly what Art meant.

"Did you do what the voice told you?" he asked.

I was curious as to why he'd asked me this esoteric question, so I turned it around and asked him the same thing, "Have you ever heard a voice?"

"Yes, I have. And something amazing happened."

Art started at the beginning. A few months earlier, as a part-time origami teacher at the LaFarge Lifelong Learning Institute in Milwaukee, he was asked to represent the school at an exhibit at a large shopping mall in the area. He decided to take along a couple hundred paper cranes that he'd folded to give to people who would stop at this booth asking questions about origami.

A week before the event, however, Art heard a strange voice. It was inside his head, loud and clear, telling him over and over to find a piece of gold foil paper and to make a golden origami crane.

At first Art ignored the voice. He was, after all, a man with both feet on the ground, not given to hearing voices or believing in such strange phenomena. But the voice continued every day with the same simple request: *Find a piece of gold foil and make a golden origami crane.*

Art harrumphed and tried to ignore the voice. But then he found himself talking back to the voice. *Why gold foil anyway? Paper is much easier to work with,* he grumbled.

The voice continued to haunt him. Art continued to grumble. Finally, the night before the event at the mall, the voice was even more insistent and more specific. *Do it! Make a crane out of gold foil paper. And tomorrow you must give the golden crane to a special person.*

By now Art was getting cranky. *What special person? This is ridiculous! How will I know who the special person is?*

The voice continued, clear as a star-filled winter sky inside his head. *You'll know who the special person is,* the voice answered stoically.

Before his commonsense voice could talk him out of it, Art went down to his basement shelves where he stored his collection of origami paper. He searched and searched until he found one piece of shiny gold foil paper six inches square.

That evening, Art slowly, carefully, painstakingly folded and shaped the unforgiving gold foil until it became as graceful and delicate as a real crane about to take flight. He packed the exquisite bird in a large box along with about two hundred colorful paper cranes he'd made over the previous few weeks.

The next day at the mall, dozens upon dozens of people stopped by Art's booth. Youngsters, their parents, middle-aged people and senior citizens all asked questions about origami. Art demonstrated the art. He folded, unfolded, refolded. He explained the intricate details, the need for sharp creases. He created different animals and unusual shapes for his audience as they strolled by.

Then, toward the end of the day, an older woman was standing in front of Art. He'd completely forgotten about the voice in his head that had bugged him during the previous week. But now suddenly he felt a warmth moving up from his toes to his eyebrows. He knew immediately that the woman standing in front of him was the special person.

Art had never seen her before, and she didn't say a word as she watched him carefully fold a bright pink piece of paper into a striking paper crane with pointed, graceful wings.

Art glanced up at her face, and before he knew what he was doing, his hands were down on the floor in the big box that contained the supply of paper cranes. There it was, the delicate gold foil bird he'd labored over the night before. He retrieved it and carefully placed it in the woman's hand.

"I don't know why, but there's been a very loud voice inside me for a week telling me that I'm supposed to give you this golden crane. The crane, by the way, is the ancient symbol of peace," Art said to the older woman.

The woman didn't say a word as she slowly cupped her

small hand around the fragile bird as if it were alive. When Art looked up at her face, he saw tears filling her eyes, ready to spill out.

Finally, the woman took a deep breath and formed her words slowly. "My husband died three weeks ago. This is the first time I've been out of the house since his funeral. Today . . . today. . . ." The woman could hardly get the words out. She wiped her eyes with her free hand, still gently cradling the golden crane with the other.

In a moment, she continued. As she looked down at the golden bird, a hint of a smile came across her lips. She spoke very quietly, "Today is our golden anniversary."

Then the woman looked directly into Art's eyes as she placed her free hand on top of Art's own. In a clear voice, she said, "Thank you for this beautiful gift. Now I know that my dear husband is at peace. Now I'm at peace. This bird, this symbol of peace, is God's messenger. Don't you see? That voice you heard. It was the voice of God, and this beautiful golden crane is a gift from the Almighty. It's the most wonderful fiftieth wedding anniversary present I could have received. Thank you for listening to the voice inside your head, to the voice of God."

That's how my friend Art learned to listen very carefully when a little voice within him tells him to do something he may not understand at the time. And that's how Art convinced me to do the same. And I've learned that when you listen very carefully, it's amazing what you'll hear.

Purple

by Lonnie Hull DuPont

SEVERAL YEARS AGO, I moved back to my home state of
Michigan after having lived out of state for the better part
of fifteen years. My husband and I purchased a pre-Civil
War farmhouse twenty miles from where I was born. Soon
after we moved, something quite unexpected happened. I
had been adopted at birth during a time when all records
pertaining to adoptions were sealed forever in the state of
Michigan and in many other states as well. As a young
adult, I had researched my biological roots, an effort that
predated the national movement to help adult adoptees
find their biological families. Through a combination of
diligence and dumb luck, I was able to locate not just one
but both of my biological parents. I met my biological
father briefly, and that's another story for another time.
But I never met my biological mother.

Her name was Elaine, and she gave birth to me in 1953,
a time when having a baby out of wedlock was covered in
shame. I believe that's why the letters I began sending to
Elaine over the years were never answered: the shame
went too deep. Even though I knew her whereabouts all

that time, I chose not to walk up to her door and introduce myself. I knew she had no other children, but what about her husband? Did he know? I took her silence to mean that she'd prefer I not intrude. And other than sending an occasional letter, I didn't. There eventually came a point when I accepted that Elaine would never answer my letters, and I stopped sending them.

A few months after moving into the farmhouse in Michigan, I came home from work one day to be met at the door by my husband, who said, "Come in, honey. I want you to sit down. I have something to tell you." After all these years, Elaine's friends were trying to reach me. Three different people from three different states all called my house on that same day to report that people were looking for me regarding my mother.

Elaine's health had been failing, and after her husband died a few months before, she had moved into assisted living. Since then, her friends had been secretly trying to locate me for weeks, never dreaming I was in the very same county. Unfortunately, they found me three days after Elaine died. She hadn't even known a search for me was in progress. Many good things came out of this find, and I thank God for that. But I was—and still am—terribly disappointed that never in this world will I meet the woman who gave birth to me and then gave me up in the hope that I would have a better life than she could offer. Never.

Elaine died on April 24, and her memorial service would

not be until May 8. In the meantime, I got to know her close friends. They showered me with pictures and mementos and stories of this woman with the lively personality. She was tremendous fun, it seemed, full of laughter, though at times her friends sensed the laughter may have been masking a deep inner pain. She enjoyed people, traveled, loved to read. The fun, the people, the travel and the voracious reading were all things we shared in common. I heard her voice on tape and recognized my own. I saw pictures of her and recognized myself. There were any number of odd details we shared in our lives and personalities, right down to possessing the very same kind of blank books to write in.

One of the things we did not share, however, was her love of the color purple—a color I've always felt looks better in nature than on fabric. When Elaine's goddaughter acquired the purple plush chair that had been Elaine's, I was not envious.

Now my life was full of amazing new facts about myself —something I suppose you can appreciate only if such information has been denied you all of your life. I knew who I was now, in all ways. I had a new extended family, a new circle of friends, and almost all the information about my background I could want. I was grateful. Nevertheless, my sadness was heavy.

The day of Elaine's memorial service was a lovely one, sunny and warm for early May. But I felt anxious that morning as I dressed, knowing that I would be meeting some biological relatives for the first time and many other people who did not yet know I existed. My husband couldn't accompany me that day, so I kissed him good-bye and headed out the door.

This was our first spring in the farmhouse and also the first time in my adult years that I had a yard. The house sat on about an acre of mowed grass, flowering bushes and maple trees. So before driving to the service that morning, I first beelined for the lilacs to see if they were in bloom. Nothing in this world is as sweet as lilacs to me, and that morning I hoped there would be blossoms to ease my sadness and anxiety. There were not. It was still too early in the season.

I turned to the driveway, and then I saw it. Our entire acre of lawn was covered in purple violets. Elaine's favorite color. And it was in nature, not on fabric. They weren't lilacs, but I chose to take them as a good sign anyway. I wanted to believe their blooming was a kind of direct comfort from God that morning. Or even a message from Elaine, assuring me that we would know one another in the next life. But I made myself brush aside such thoughts as more wistful than realistic. I should just be happy to discover we had violets at our house.

At the memorial service, the minister read Elaine's confirmation verse: "Make a joyful noise unto the Lord," and everyone who knew her laughed out loud. Her friends read a poem that even included her love of purple. It was a fitting service. I was introduced as Elaine's daughter, and while it made me feel very good to be acknowledged in that way, I still felt that disappointment. But at least I had this wonderful new batch of relatives and friends. And life moved along.

The years go by. I think of Elaine often. I especially think of her in the spring, partly because that's when she died and partly because I so vividly remember that blanket of purple violets that popped up in my yard on the day of her memorial service. And now I believe those violets were indeed the message of comfort I needed that day. Because in all the springs since then, I've continued to live in the farmhouse, and I never again saw a violet in my yard. Not one.

Letters from Another Time

by Dorothy Corson

M Y FATHER WAS A VERY RESERVED Canadian of English origin. Though he was a sensitive, loving parent, he wasn't a man to express his deepest feelings. Dad died almost twenty years ago, but often since, I've felt a twinge of yearning . . . I didn't remember him ever saying "I love you."

Recently, my son asked me to show him how to letter a title on the folder for a school assignment. "Oh, I wish your grandfather were here," I exclaimed, shaking my head. "He had an unusual way of lettering his blueprints. He even showed me how simple it was to do. But I've forgotten the trick of it."

For hours afterward, I racked my brain, trying to remember how Dad formed those simple, distinctive letters; but all I could summon up was a nostalgic image of him bending over his drawing board.

The next day my brother stopped by unexpectedly. He handed me a worn, folded envelope. "I was helping Mother sort through some of Dad's old papers, and we found this.

Looks like something Dad must have done for you. We thought you'd like to have it."

When I unfolded the envelope, I felt a shiver of excitement. On it before me, in Dad's special lettering, was a complete alphabet, the very one I'd wanted to show my son.

It was like a message sent from heaven.

But even more thrilling was the notation at the bottom in my father's familiar hand: "This what you want, Dot?" And, alongside it, framed in a diamond, three words, words that were a long time in the coming, but not too late to warm me for the rest of my life: "I love you."

PART X

Assurance of Remembrance

As a father pities his children,
So the Lord pities those who fear Him.
For He knows our frame;
He remembers that we are dust.

Psalm 103:13–14 NKJV

WE ALL WANT TO BE REMEMBERED by those we love. The Bible assures us that God remembers us, even in our sorrows. And the men and women whose stories appear in this section explain the comfort they've received from sensing the watchful presence of family members or friends who have preceded them in death. A dream. A music box. A voice. A music collection. A windswept bonnet. Each gives assurance of a familiar and comforting presence. As you read, may you feel the love of God who knows your grief, who remembers that you are like a vulnerable child in need of loving-kindness and care.

The Music Box

by Shirley Miller

M Y HOBBY IS COLLECTING MUSIC BOXES—nothing expensive or rare or old, just music boxes I like and enjoy listening to. For years, my mother's favorite was a figurine of an old woman sitting in a rocking chair and holding a few balloons.

Every time my mother came to visit me, she would go into the den and look at the music box and smile thoughtfully. Then she'd say, "If Pa goes first, that's me—sitting on a rocking chair in Lincoln Park, selling balloons." We would laugh. Then she would push the button and listen to the song it played: "Try to Remember" from *The Fantasticks*.

Mother, then approaching eighty, suffered a mild stroke that put her in the hospital for a week. After that, she never became completely well again. Gradually, her weakness increased. My father, who had been retired for several years, now became Mother's constant attendant. My sister and I took turns going over one day a week to shop, clean house and prepare casseroles and stews that my father could warm up for their meals.

Often my mother would ask me, "How's the old lady with the balloons?"

"Fine," I'd say. "She asks about you all the time." And we'd laugh.

In October my phone rang very early one morning. It was my father. He said, "Honey, you'd better get over here. It's Ma."

"What happened?" I asked, fearing the worst.

"She fell getting out of bed," he said. "I don't have the strength to lift her."

"I'll be right there," I said. I called my sister, told her the bad news and said I'd pick her up on the way.

We found Mother sitting on the floor in her room, resting against her bed. Her face was sad and helpless, with tears of humiliation in her eyes. We got her back in bed.

"I'm sorry this happened," she whispered. "Thanks for coming. I'll make it up to you."

Those were her last words to us.

I called the doctor. An ambulance was there in minutes, but on the way to the hospital, Mother lost consciousness. She was put into intensive care, while out in the waiting room the doctor told us, "It's very bad. There's been a lot of brain damage. She may not come out of this."

It was the beginning of a long ordeal for all of us. Mother went into a coma. Ten days later she was transferred to a private room, where we could stay with her all day. Dad left the room frequently for a cigarette, his pain a constant frown on his face.

I was there every day, all day. Mother remained in a coma, but I talked to her anyway, hoping she could somehow hear me. "We're all praying for you, Ma," I told her, "everybody—even the old lady with the balloons."

Early in the morning on November 19, with our house still in darkness, the phone rang. I braced myself, "Hello?"

"Mrs. Miller, this is the head nurse at the hospital. I'm sorry to have to tell you that your mother died ten minutes ago."

Even though I had been expecting them, her words were like a blow. "Thank you," I managed to say somehow. "I'll take care of everything." As I hung up, I glanced at the clock. It was 5:10 AM. My mother had died at five, after being in a coma for forty-nine days.

Somehow we all made it through the next few days. Then came the strain of adjusting to the loss, of waiting for the sorrow to fade. Time passed, but the sorrow did not disappear. When death takes a loved one, even though you trust in the promise of everlasting life, something in you longs for reassurance, for proof of that promise. It's only human, I guess.

The months went by. One season slipped into another. One day, my husband, Lenny, came home from work with a bad cold. I suggested that he spend a couple of days in bed, but he said he had too much work to do at the office and couldn't spare the time. A few days later, the cold was so bad that he had no choice. I nursed him all day, and then, so he could sleep undisturbed, I spent the night on the sofa in the den.

It had been a hard day for me because it was the day before the first anniversary of Mother's death. I kept thinking about her, missing her, wishing she were only a telephone call away. It would have been so helpful just to talk to her, ask her advice about Lenny, feel the warmth and reassurance she always gave.

Tired and worried about Lenny, I tossed fitfully on the sofa for a while. I kept thinking about all the uncertainties of life, and I felt lost and lonely somehow. I missed our familiar bed and Lenny's comforting presence. Finally I drifted off into a restless sleep.

Hours later I awoke with a start; something strange, something unfamiliar had wakened me. For a moment I didn't know what it was. Then I heard the music. The soft sounds of a familiar song drifted through my mind. But where was it coming from? There was darkness all around me. Had I been dreaming it? No, the music was still playing. In the darkness I could still hear its eerie tinkling.

I sat up. I stared into the gloom. There, on the desk, was the silhouette of the old lady with the balloons, and the song I heard coming from the music box was my mother's favorite, "Try to Remember."

"But it can't be playing," I said to myself. "Nobody's

touched it. And the last time I played that box, I distinctly remember letting it run down!"

And then I remembered what day it was. November 19. I glanced at the desk clock. It was 5:00 AM. Ma had died exactly one year ago to the day, to the hour, to the minute! I began to cry. I whispered to the dark: "If that's you, Ma, I hope you're safe and happy. You know that we still love you and miss you and, yes, we still remember."

I lay down again, weeping, listening to the music until it stopped, and I fell asleep, reassured at last.

I awoke again around 7:30 AM and smelled bacon. I got up and went to the kitchen. There was Lenny, shaved, fully dressed, at the stove frying bacon and eggs. "You were so sound asleep that I decided to fix breakfast myself," he said. "I'm going to work."

I stared at him, astonished. "Are you well enough for that?"

"Yes," he said. "During the night, the cold just seemed to melt out of me. I feel great."

I felt as if I was going to cry again. "I'll do that," I said. I took the spatula away from Lenny and turned my back to him, close to tears.

Lenny went to the table and sat down to his cup of coffee. He said, "Tell me something. Did I hear you playing Ma's music box during the night, or did I dream it?"

I fought the tears. I couldn't talk about it yet.

"No," I said. "I didn't play it."

And in my heart I thanked the Lord for using a little mechanical music box to let us know that our mother was safe with Him, that she still loved us, still missed us, and, yes, still remembered.

Never Too Late

by Dave Fronczak

WHEN I WAS GROWING UP, my father was an alcoholic. It was risky having friends over; Dad might come home and pass out on the couch, his breath reeking of whiskey. I tried to make him happy, but nothing I did was ever good enough. Even at age twelve, when I started working almost every waking hour after classes to help pay the family's bills, in his bleary eyes I was a sissy because I wasn't a sports star at school as he had been.

Finally, spending two years battling tuberculosis sobered him up. By then I had married my high school sweetheart Joanne and had two kids of my own, Walter and Debbie. I worked at a car repair shop, which I dreamed of owning someday. I thought maybe I would at last get to know my father, that I'd be able to let go of all the unhappy memories. But soon after his recovery, doctors discovered that a lifetime of working in foundries had left Dad with a more serious lung disease called silicosis. Doctors feared he had only five years left to live, at most.

Five years to make up for my entire childhood and to get

to know his grandchildren. *It's not fair,* I thought over and over. Still, in that time Dad developed a bond with six-year-old Walter, bestowing on him all the attention he'd never been able to give me when I was a boy. I was pleased. But I couldn't understand why God had waited till Dad was dying to show me what a good father he could have been.

I spent as much time with Dad as I could. We had real conversations, talking about my work, my family, sports—anything but the past. I just couldn't bring myself to mention it now that he was so ill.

One evening I went over to Dad's house to play some poker.

"Where's the kid?" he asked, patting me on the shoulder in greeting. He always asked after Walter like that.

"Here, Grandpa!" Walter burst in, and Dad scooped him up in his massive arms. I wished I could turn back the clock and be a little boy in Dad's arms again, that I could see his eyes light up that way for me.

We sat in high-backed wooden chairs at the kitchen table, and I dealt the cards as Walter played with the buttons on Dad's shirt.

"Son, I got the workers' comp money yesterday," said Dad quietly, as he picked up his cards. "I'd like you to have some of it so you can buy the shop."

I nearly dropped my hand. "What?"

"I figure it's the least I can . . . well, I figure you deserve it." He turned his head to the side, coughing a little, and then ruffled Walter's hair. I was speechless.

No, my father hadn't come out and said he was sorry, but he was showing me he cared. Still, I longed for him to say some magic words to take away all the hurt. Why couldn't I just let go of the past?

I threw myself into running my new business. Meanwhile, Dad was in and out of the hospital. Even though Walter wasn't allowed to visit him in his room, Dad made us bring him to the parking lot. "Where's the kid?" he'd ask and I'd point. Walter would jump up and down yelling "Grandpa!" and Dad would push himself up in bed and wave and smile through his window.

Early on a chilly Sunday morning, a nurse called me at work and said Dad was in pretty bad shape. *It's too soon*, I thought as I sped down the highway. There was so much I wanted to talk about, so much more I needed from him. But by the time I got there, he was gone. Shuffling out of the hospital into the blinding sunlight, I felt like a boy my son's age, not a twenty-nine-year-old father. It was July 20, 1969, the day of the first moon landing, but glancing up at the sky through my tears, I could think only of Dad looking down on me and yelling, "Don't be a sissy!" Would I always think only of the bad things?

After the funeral, I took my family to a friend's cottage on Sugar Island in the St. Mary's River for a little time off. The fifth day of our trip, I trudged down the steep hillside to the river just after dawn and splashed my face with the ice-cold water. As I set up a folding chair, Walter appeared with his inner tube.

"Can I play here, Daddy?"

"Okay, Son, just stay close to shore." I lounged back with a pair of binoculars, listening to the low rush of the waves and the whistling birds as I switched my attention back and forth between Walter and the Soo Locks canal system in the distance. Walter lay on his stomach on the inner tube, his toes just grazing the water.

Shifting the binoculars, I tried to make out the name on a big ore boat passing through the locks. I checked on Walter and then squinted again at the locks. I stood up to get a better look. "Where's the kid?" asked a clear, familiar voice behind me. Instinctively I swung the binoculars back toward the river. Walter's inner tube was being borne swiftly away on the current. Where was he?

Dropping the binoculars, I sprinted toward the river. "Walter! Walter!" I leapt into the waves. Reaching around madly in the water, I cursed myself for taking my eyes off him even for a second. *Dear God, help!* I caught sight of an outline against the sandy river bottom. Walter! I dove and lifted him under the arms and held him close to my chest as we rose to the surface. He wasn't breathing.

"Help!" I cried frantically as I ran up the hill to the cottage, Walter's small frame bouncing against my shoulder. Then I heard him cough. I laid him on the grass and pushed aside the blond curls matted against his pale forehead. He clutched my arm. "Daddy . . . Dad . . . ," he sputtered, trying to say something.

"Quiet now, Son. You just rest." I wrapped him in my jacket and carried him inside.

On the drive back home that evening, my wife and I were quiet as the kids rested in the backseat. I let my eyes follow the distant twinkling lights along the Mackinac Bridge and then glanced up at the rising moon. "Joanne, I have to tell you something," I said softly, "something incredible. At the river today I heard a voice." My spine tingled at the memory. "It was my dad's."

Walter leaned forward between the front seats, grabbing my shoulder. "Daddy, that's what I was trying to tell you before. I saw Grandpa in the water today! I was so scared until he came and taught me how to hold my breath and do water tricks."

Tears filled my eyes, but this time I didn't think of my dad scolding me, only of the gentle, concerned voice I'd heard at the river, the voice that quieted my angry memories. God had sent an angel who looked like Dad to comfort my son in those terrifying moments. And He had let me hear my father say the most precious words imaginable —words that had saved my son.

Coached from Heaven

by Bob Simms

I MET RICK DERBY at my son's first Little League practice. It was a brisk spring day, and all the youngsters clam-
ored for the positions they wanted to play. "Coach, let me
be shortstop!" "I want to play first base!" Rick listened to
every kid and managed to accommodate each one.

To my surprise, my own seven-year-old Korey begged to
pitch. "Sure!" Rick said. The assistant coach, I went out to
the field to show the other boys how to shag pop flies,
while Rick ushered Korey onto the mound and watched
him.

"The kid's got some talent," Rick confided. "He'll do
well." Rick and I both worked for Boeing. We were in different departments and never saw each other around. But
now that we had the Bridgeton Bulldogs in common, we
began e-mailing each other at work. In his typically upbeat
fashion he wrote, "1994 is going to be our year!"

But the season got off to a shaky start. Not one of the
boys got a hit in the first game. Most kids didn't even make
contact. Rick was not to be discouraged. "Hey, Bob," he
exclaimed as I stood up from the bench, "did you see our

boys play?" Without waiting for my answer, he went on, "Every single one of them showed up and every one of them fielded. That's two out of three. Not bad, not bad at all!" I had to hand it to him. Rick was taking the long view.

The second game, he asked Korey to pitch. He knelt down in the dugout at the Bridgeton Ball Field, looked Korey in the eye and said, "So, what can you do for me, son?" Korey shrugged, adjusted his cap and sauntered up to the mound like a veteran. He squinted at the batter, looked to Coach Rick for the signal, wound up and threw the ball.

What happened next was disastrous. The batter knocked the ball straight back at Korey. It hit him in the shoulder and sent him reeling. Both Rick and I ran to the mound. Fighting back tears, Korey insisted he was okay. He finished the inning but came back to the dugout saying he never wanted to pitch again.

Yet Coach Rick never gave up. He worked with Korey in practices, always encouraging and praising. He kept Korey's name on the roster as a pitcher. "So, what can you do for me?" Rick would say. At times it really frustrated me. *Just tell him what you want him to do,* I thought. *You're the coach. You're in charge.* But that wasn't his way. Rick believed that the kids should decide what they wanted to do in a game. The league was for them, not the parents and not the coaches.

By our fourth season we had a winning team, and Korey was back on the mound. By then, I'd adopted a lot of

Coach Rick's ways. You could hear me yelling from the bench, "Awesome hit! Great catch! What a pitch!" I was awfully proud of our team and especially proud of Korey. I'd watch Rick sidle up to my son in the dugout and say, "So, what can you do for me?" Korey would shrug, scratch his head, put on his mitt and head out to the mound. And he'd pitch a darn good game.

At season's end, we were tied for first. Our last game before playoffs was on a Thursday night. Wednesday afternoon Rick e-mailed me, "Can't make the game tomorrow. I'm in Seattle on business. Let's win so we can play St. Ann next week."

It was a magical game. Everything happened just right. Korey pitched a couple of beautiful innings, and he hit a triple in the bottom of the seventh. We came away with a solid victory and a berth in the playoffs. As we were walking to our car, Korey exclaimed, "My biggest hit of the whole season, and Rick missed it!"

The next day I received the horrifying news: In his hotel room in Seattle, Rick had a fatal stroke.

I drove home early from work. Korey was in the family room, playing a game on the computer. "Son," I said, "I have some very sad news. Coach Rick is dead." Korey jumped up from his chair and grabbed me. "You're lying to me. You've never lied to me before, but this time you're lying." He fell into my arms, sobbing.

For several days, Korey didn't want to do anything. He

didn't touch his baseball glove. We went to the funeral and saw that Rick was much more than a terrific coach. He was a good friend, a leader in his church, and a dedicated husband and father. Korey came home and read the Bible. *Lord, give him some comfort*, I prayed.

Our game against St. Ann was postponed a couple of times, but finally we had to face it, and Korey had to face pitching without Rick. Both teams played their best, and Korey pitched well, but even after two extra innings, the game was still tied. The light had drained from the sky when the umpires called it a draw. Rick would have said the tie meant everybody won. Korey seemed relieved the game was over. "You know, Dad," he said, "I think I miss Rick most when I'm on the pitcher's mound."

For months, Korey was stricken with anxiety. He sometimes called me at the office just to talk. If I was away from my desk, he had me paged. Evenings he followed me around the house like a puppy. Once I refused to go on a business trip because of Korey. He was afraid I would die, afraid I would disappear like his beloved coach Rick.

When baseball season started up again, Korey agreed to play, but he refused to pitch. A couple of times I raised the issue. Nothing doing. Korey wouldn't pitch.

Then a cool breeze was coming off the river one spring day, blowing up little clouds of dust. We were playing St. Ann, the same team we'd faced right after Rick's death. I was in the dugout, assigning positions to the boys, when to my amazement Korey walked out to the mound, ready to pitch. I looked at him. He smiled. "Korey's our starting pitcher today," I said.

He pitched a complete game, displaying the natural talent Rick had recognized from the beginning, and we won. *Korey's going to be all right*, I thought.

After accepting a row of high fives, Korey ambled off the field and sat on the bench next to me. "So, Korey, what made you want to pitch again?"

"I heard him, Dad," he said. "It was just like it used to be. That same voice telling me I was doing great. And then those same words: 'So, Korey, what can you do for me?' Somehow Rick doesn't seem all that far away."

I supposed he wasn't. Rick was with God in heaven, which meant he was as close as an angel's message to a hurting young boy. As Korey and I walked out to the car, I glanced back at the pitcher's mound. Even heaven has its baseball fans.

He Makes Winds His Messengers

by Ann Shane

ALBERT AND I STOOD on our balcony together, admiring the lush spring greenery. "You're beautiful," my husband said, as he had so many times during our sixty years together.

That summer Albert died of a heart attack. For weeks after, although exhausted, I couldn't sleep. I saw an old lady with messy hair and dark eyes in the mirror. *Albert wouldn't even recognize you*, I thought, and I made an appointment at the beauty parlor.

By the time my face, hair and nails were done, I felt like the beautiful woman Albert loved. Rain poured outside, so I bought a bonnet before I left the salon. On my way to the car, the bonnet flew off my head and into the sky. My hair was drenched, my makeup ran. I felt so foolish for having gone through all that trouble, and for what? I skipped the beauty parlor the next week, and the week after that.

Then one autumn day, I stood on our balcony and watched the falling leaves dance in the wind. I felt like one of them, forgotten, old. *God, now that Albert's gone, who sees me, a lonely old woman trying to look pretty?* I was just about to go inside when something else floated down to join the dead leaves and then, twisting with life, climbed higher into the sky. Slowly, gently, it came to rest at my feet. My lost bonnet had returned, a whisper from heaven saying, "I do."

PART XI

Symbols of Blessing

O my God, my soul is cast down within me;
Therefore I will remember You from the land
of the Jordan. . . .
Deep calls unto deep at the noise of Your waterfalls;
All Your waves and billows have gone over me.
The Lord will command His loving-kindness
in the daytime,
And in the night His song shall be with me.

Psalm 42:6–8 NKJV

"DEEP CALLS UNTO DEEP." It's a poetic phrase that acknowledges an anguished yearning symbolically tied to the wonders of nature. Then, in the very next sentence, the psalmist writes of God's loving-kindness and comforting song: 'round-the-clock blessings.

When surprised by specific sights and sounds—many of them from nature's realm—the authors in this section sense they've received a sign of blessing, a symbol that represents a connection between this world and the world beyond time. No noisy waterfalls are represented here, but butterflies, hawks, tomatoes, a soldier's ring . . . items discovered and endowed with meaning that comforted one grieving heart and can speak to us as well.

Fourth-of-July Butterfly

by Maddie Merrifield

*E*ARLY ON THAT INDEPENDENCE DAY morning nine years ago, I could already smell the grills being started in people's backyards. Kids down the street were decorating their bikes for the parade. A neighbor was loading up his truck with folding chairs for our church picnic. That night there would be fireworks.

It should have been a happy time for my family, gathering to celebrate the wedding of my twenty-two-year-old daughter Karen two days later. At the same time, my twenty-five-year-old daughter Nancy had been given a one-day pass so she could leave the psychiatric facility where she was being treated for depression and spend this afternoon with us. I pressed my fingers against my lips to keep from crying. *Dear God*, I wondered, *how can I possibly get through all this?*

I looked into the yard where my husband Bob was replacing a burned-out floodlight by the back door. As he removed the old bulb, the fixture wobbled and out fluttered a huge butterfly. Its wingspan must have been four inches. It rose in the air, circled the yard, and with a swoop came to rest on our welcome mat on the back porch. "Bob," I cried, "I just can't believe it!"

My mind raced back to my grandfather's funeral many years ago. That day our family had stood with arms around one another reminiscing outside the barbershop Grandpa had owned. All of a sudden a butterfly landed on the shop door. Grandmother gasped. "It's a sign," she said. Grandma explained that she and Grandpa had asked God to send a butterfly when one of them reached heaven safely.

The next important butterfly to appear in my life came shortly after my father's death. I was fifteen and working at a doughnut shop that difficult summer. One evening when Mom met me to walk home, she gestured excitedly at the shop's screen door. An enormous butterfly had landed there. Holding my breath, I scooped it into my hands. I carried it all the way home. When released, it lingered on the railing of our porch for perhaps an hour until abruptly spreading its wings and lifting off into the night sky.

I grew up, married and had two daughters, and butterflies continued to be symbols of reassurance and hope to us all. We gave one another butterfly cards, stationery and jewelry. Once, during a rough patch in our lives, a butterfly landed on the steering wheel of Mom's car and another atop a golf ball my husband had been about to hit.

When Mom died in late November a few years back, we had already experienced several New England frosts. My sister and I walked through the woods on the morning of our mother's death. A yellow butterfly suddenly appeared in the chilly air and danced in front of my sister before it darted off. Within minutes a second yellow butterfly fluttered before me from a different direction.

Soon after that, my phone rang with a message from my brother, "You'll never guess what I just saw," he said. "A yellow butterfly!"

And now it was the Fourth of July, and I was staring at yet another butterfly. As I carefully pulled the welcome mat to a safe place on the side of the porch, it didn't budge. Several hours later it was still there, motionless. Was it injured? Sick? Dying?

Karen, the bride-to-be, appeared, flushed with excitement. "Here, honey," I said, "this must be a special sign for you." Karen looked at the butterfly, its wings trembling in the summer air. "It's not for me, Mom," Karen said. "It's for Nancy." We picked up the butterfly and carried it into the kitchen, where it circled the room before alighting on the windowsill by the sink.

Karen's fiancé Paul had driven Nancy home from the hospital, and as the car pulled up, we rushed to meet her. "Nancy!" Putting my arm around my daughter, I drew Nancy into the kitchen and was telling her how glad we were to see her when I saw her eyes widen and her pale face light up. "A butterfly!" she exclaimed.

She went to the sink and slowly put out her hand. As if

on cue, the butterfly left the sill and moved directly onto Nancy's finger, where it sat with wings fully spread.

"You'll never believe it," Nancy said, her voice a whisper over her tears, "but I've been praying that a butterfly would sit on my finger as a sign that I'll get well. People told me that I could wait for a hundred years and it would never happen—that I was asking for a miracle." She looked at the butterfly resting on her finger, and then at us, eyes shining. "But there are miracles."

We stayed there in the kitchen a long time, getting caught up on Nancy's progress and Karen's wedding preparations. Then Nancy took the butterfly outside and held it aloft. Saying farewell, we all watched it fly across the garden and into the woods.

That evening more family members arrived to share laughter, hugs and hot dogs. We lit sparklers in the twilight, and when fireworks burst from the darkness, we all stood with arms around one another, looking upward into the sky. Once again we would face the future together, borne on the wings of a promise that had sustained our family for generations.

Soldier's Ring

by Thomas Fleming

ONE OCTOBER DAY LAST YEAR I received a telephone call from Jersey City, my hometown. I had grown up there— just across the Hudson River from New York City—as the son of a celebrated local politician. "Did you ever lose a gold ring in France?" asked my friend Kenneth French, the director of the New Jersey Room in the public library.

"Yes, years ago," I said, surprised and curious. "But I never expect to see it again."

"Well, Tom, hold on to your hat. A Frenchman has found your ring."

For at least fifteen seconds, I was unable to speak. The ring had originally belonged to my father. He gave it to me a few months before his death in 1957. Eleven years later, though, I lost it in France's Argonne Forest, where my father and his fellow doughboys of 1918 had fought in one of the biggest battles in American history and where I had gone in 1968 on a pilgrimage both professional and personal.

Ken explained that Gil Malmasson, the young man who had found the ring, had tracked me down by searching the

Internet for the names in the ring's inscription: "From Mayor Frank Hague to Sheriff Teddy Fleming, 1945." A Jersey City Web site contained brief biographies of Hague and other former mayors. My friend was delighted to discover that the Web site had connected Jersey City with a major episode in American history. The ring linked me with that history too—but it also reunited me with my father in a powerful and mysterious way and forced me to examine my own place in the world as a father. Forty-one years after his death, I felt him reaching out to me. What was he saying?

To find the answer to that question, I decided I had to go back to France and ask Gil Malmasson to put the ring on my finger in the exact place where I had lost it in 1968.

As my wife Alice and I flew across the Atlantic a few weeks after Ken's amazing call, my mind was flooded with memories. For more than a week during that cold, bleak March of 1968, I had ridden and hiked around the Argonne with the battle diary of my father's regiment, the 312th Infantry of the 78th Division, in my hand. At the time I was preparing an article for the fiftieth anniversary of the battle for *American Heritage* magazine.

I followed Sergeant Teddy Fleming and his fellow doughboys in their struggle across the hellish landscape of that vast valley. In my mind's eye, I saw them pounded from three sides by German artillery while machine guns spewed death from woods and blockhouses and trenches.

The Argonne's small towns and farms had changed little in fifty years. Just as I read in the diary, "Today we attacked La Ferme Rouge" (The Red Farm), Alice and I rounded a curve and there was the slope-roofed farmhouse, still a weathered red. A burly farmer named André Godart met us at the door and told us he had been there when the doughboys drove the Germans from the trenches and blockhouses that ringed the farm.

Godart led us to a nearby woods, the Bois des Loges, where the Americans took heavy casualties. He told us in somber tones how, as a boy of sixteen, he had helped carry the dead and dying soldiers after the Germans retreated. Then he took us back to his farmhouse and poured refreshments. Raising his glass, he said, "To the son of the man who freed the Bois des Loges!"

Never had I felt so proud of my father, or so close to him. The ring on my finger played a part in this. It was a reminder, guaranteeing my ability to trace his change from being a son of struggling Irish immigrants to becoming a leader of men.

During the closing week of the battle, Sergeant Teddy Fleming won a lieutenant's commission for his reliability and courage. Becoming an officer was a remarkable accomplishment for a man whose education had ended in the eighth grade. It became the springboard for his successful career as a political leader in Jersey City, a career the ring crowned.

But then came my scarifying moment of loss in France. Driving along a road, we stopped beside a marker telling us that in the nearby ravine, the 77th Division's "Lost Battalion" held out for five days when the Germans cut them off in the first phase of the battle. I decided to slide down the steep embankment to explore the site.

After about ten minutes of prowling among collapsed trenches and the remains of foxholes, I scrambled back up the embankment to where Alice and our driver were waiting. I had to grasp at tufts of grass and small bushes to make my way.

I glanced down at my hand. The ring was gone! Frantically I pawed at the shifting dirt. Alice joined me, but it was useless. I was not even sure where it had fallen off. Alice said sadly, "Tom, if it's any consolation, a part of your father will always be a part of this battlefield."

Those were my memories as we landed in Paris in 1998. Young Gil Malmasson met us at the airport with a reporter and a photographer. The French media saw rich historical meaning in the ring. It was a symbol of the long friendship between France and America.

For me, the personal meaning remained foremost. The next day—the day before Thanksgiving—we drove to the Argonne. A French TV crew filmed us. We stood above the very ravine where I had lost the ring.

During the drive to the battlefield, I had asked Gil why he had been drawn to the hobby of searching historic sites with a metal detector. "When I find something like your father's ring on a battlefield," he'd said, "I'm helping myself and others to remember that even here, where death seemed supreme, there are living men who have personal stories to tell."

As Gil slipped the ring onto my finger, his words gathered force in my mind. The memory of Teddy Fleming's courage and caring, both as a soldier and a father, was being reborn.

An officer and a father have a lot in common. Both have to be firm and often tough, but fair. Above all, they have to prove they care about the people in their charge. On the wall in his bedroom, my father had two poems in simple frames. One, "My Buddy," was an elegy for a pal killed in action. The other was "In Flanders Fields," with its unforgettable opening lines:

> In Flanders fields the poppies blow
> Between the crosses, row on row.

I remembered the times when Teddy Fleming was there for me as a father. When I was an eleven-year-old third baseman, a hot smash took a bad hop and hit me in the teeth. Blood flowed. I ran home, certain I was fatally injured. (Even at that age I had a writer's vivid imagination.)

My father was on his way to an important political meeting. He was wearing a homburg and one of his best suits. He wiped off the blood, prodded my teeth and assured me I was going to live. "But we can't let this spook you," he declared.

He called the man who was running the meeting and said he would be late. Then he peeled off his coat, threw his hat aside and took me out to the backyard. He started hitting grounders to me. I jerked my head away at first. "Keep your head down," he encouraged.

He hit the ball harder and harder. In half an hour I'd learned to keep my head down, fielding his hardest shots. A few years later, I had become one of the better third basemen in Jersey City.

Once, when I was sixteen, I was in the Jersey City Medical Center awaiting a serious operation the following morning. I was sure I was doomed. About seven o'clock that night, my father showed up and told me to get dressed.

We left the hospital, and he drove us to a dinner for the Democratic chieftains of New Jersey. He took me around the room and introduced me to them, saying, "Look at this kid. He's going under the knife tomorrow morning, and he's as cool as a cucumber." The politicians shook my hand and said, "You've got your old man's nerve." By the end of the evening, I had decided maybe they were right. I went back to the hospital and slept beautifully all night.

The most poignant memory the ring evoked was a time I clashed with my father. We were on a car trip and I was reading a book instead of admiring the scenery. The man of action found it hard to comprehend this son who was so interested in mere words. He spoke sharply to me, wondering if I appreciated the time he was investing in the trip.

For a moment, I only knew how little time I thought he spent with us compared to the thousands of hours he devoted to politics. "What do you care what I'm doing?" I said. "You don't love me."

The brakes screamed and the car careened off the road. My father sprang out and paced in a field, rubbing his eyes. I could not believe it. The hero who had fought his way through the Argonne was weeping.

"You said I don't love you," he sobbed. "My family is all I've got."

That was the innermost memory of the Argonne ring, the ultimate revelation of my father's caring. I would return to it time and again for renewal as I coped with my own struggles as a father. It repeatedly inspired me to balance the demands of a writer's career with my love for my three sons and my daughter.

As I touched the ring on my finger that November day in the Argonne—the ring I had never expected to see again —I heard my father saying: "You give it the best that is in you. Your kids know you love them and your country and your God." Now I find myself believing that those thoughts, those memories, the whole experience, were gifts from heaven.

The Hawk

by Wolfgang Krismanits

I LOOKED AT THE WORDS carved into the granite headstone: "Sonja Theresa Krismanits, 1929–1970." My mother.
Just six weeks earlier, she had been fixing my tie and
straightening my cap on the morning of my high school
graduation. Nine days later, she died of a cerebral hemor-
rhage. Just like that, nothing made sense anymore. Every
morning since, I'd biked to the large, wooded cemetery to be
alone with Mom and my thoughts and to watch the birds.
But I was as confused as ever. Why had God taken someone
so good, in the prime of her life, with a husband and four
kids who needed her? I stared at the tombstone, searching
for some explanation. *Maybe there aren't any answers*, I
thought.

The expensive binoculars Mom and Dad had given me
for graduation hung around my neck. I trained them on a
flurry of blackbirds passing overhead. Watching birds used
to make me feel peaceful, but now their smooth flight only
made me anxious. I couldn't imagine ever feeling free again.

Sure, I still went through the motions. My job as a
lifeguard at a local public pool put money in the bank for

college. I had planned to go to a school in Illinois in the fall to study wildlife conservation, but that seemed trivial after my crash course in loss. I couldn't get excited about anything anymore. I always felt removed from whatever was going on, so I took every chance I could to be by myself. "This is the beginning of the rest of your life," they'd told us at graduation. The prospect was mind-numbing. The sad years stretched out like a long, deserted road before me— a whole lifetime to grieve for my mother. *Will it ever get better, God? Help me to feel something besides this pain.*

A high-pitched screech made me jump. I whisked the binoculars away from my eyes and looked around. There in an old oak tree was a large red-tailed hawk. Its wingspan must have been more than four feet. Again it shrieked, the sound bouncing off the stately maples and pines surrounding the cemetery. I wanted to cry out like that, to loosen the knot of sorrow inside me—but it was too deep, too tangled. The hawk cocked its head from side to side; then it looked at me with sharp eyes as yellow as any sun ray. I'd never seen a hawk with the distinctive markings this one had on its body. It was a magnificent find—and I hadn't even been looking for it. I focused on it and took a step closer. The bird gave a quick nod and then flew away. *Oh well.*

When I awoke the next morning, I peered out my bedroom window at the giant brushstroke of crimson across the horizon. *I wish you were still here to see the sunrise, Mom,* I thought. She had loved dawn—on family camping trips she was the first one up, frying bacon and humming softly or singing a hymn. I threw on a T-shirt and jeans and pedaled down to the cemetery. The chilly morning mist perfectly suited my mood.

I got off my bike and walked to Mom's grave. Dropping to my knees before it, I laid my head on the cold stone. When I looked up, I caught my breath. The hawk.

It stood on the same perch as the day before. I recognized the markings on its belly. *That's weird,* I thought. *Never saw a hawk around here before, and now this one two days in a row. Just another thing that doesn't make sense.* The bird stared at me, again moving its head from side to side. I mimicked its movements, trying to keep its attention. I even moved a couple of steps closer. Then, all at once, it looked up, gave a mighty flap of its wings, and lifted into the air.

That night I checked my field guide. Hawks not fully mature had those markings—apparently the one I'd seen was still young.

The following day I had been in the cemetery barely a minute when he appeared again. There was no doubt it was the same bird. *This is incredible.* I peered through my binoculars right into his piercing eyes. He stared back at me, seemingly as fascinated with me as I was with him. I managed several steps toward the tree before he flew away. *Maybe I could get him to perch on my arm,* I thought. It was a crazy idea. After all, I was eighteen years old with no experience handling birds, and hawks are creatures of the wild with razor-sharp talons that could rip me to shreds. But a vision was forming in my mind, an image of me and the hawk eye to eye. For the first time since Mom's death, I actually wanted something.

The next morning, I sped to the cemetery, a slice of bologna in my pocket. My plan was simple: I would work backward from the oak tree, placing meat closer and closer to the tombstone each day, as I approached closer and closer from the other side. My hands clenched the handle-bars as I rode. *Can this really work?*

At the cemetery, I hopped off my bike and waited. Right on schedule, the hawk winged into view. "Hi there, Red," I called. He turned to me. I waved the bologna in the air, placed it at the base of the tree, then retreated. He cocked his head and then spread his wings and swooped down, landing beside the meat. He eyed it from all angles and pecked at it twice. Finally he caught it in his beak and rose up to his perch. He elegantly threw back his head and swallowed the meat. *Yes!* In a blur, he flew off. "Good, Red," I yelled after him. On the way home, I reviewed the specifics of my plan over and over. Should I take one or two steps closer each day? Should I increase the amount of meat? How soon could I get him close enough?

My anticipation grew with each success. When I wasn't with the hawk, I was thinking about him. I found myself going to the cemetery each morning as much to see Red as to see my mother's grave. It was a project, a challenge—but something more too. I felt an intense connection to Red. I couldn't explain it. Something crucial was happening—but it was beyond my understanding.

After two weeks, Red and I were eyeing each other from only ten feet apart, the tombstone between us. He got so close I could feel the breeze from his wings as he pushed away from the ground.

One hot, muggy August morning I knew it was time. I wore a flannel shirt and tied a suede jacket around my waist. Sweat ran down my back under my heavy outfit, but if Red did come to me, I would need protection from his talons. I planned to wrap the jacket around my forearm when I got close. My heart raced faster than my pedaling feet as I neared the cemetery. A prayer pulsed through me: *Please let him come to me, God. Please let him come.*

Red was already perched on his branch. Carefully, I placed two slices of bologna on the tombstone. He stared. With each passing second, my hopes sagged. Then he spread his wings and swooped down in a gentle arc, landing on the stone directly in front of me. He was the most amazing creature I had ever seen, from his tremendous claws clinging to the stone like grappling hooks to the wavy rust-colored lines across his wings to the delicate feathers crowning his head.

This is it. I knelt and put my right forearm against the

stone. Then I held my breath, staring into his eyes. I'd never wanted anything as much as I wanted Red to take one more step. The rest of the world seemed to fall away. Looking up, he shuffled his feet on the stone. He glanced at the meat and then at me, spreading his wings. *Oh, no, he's flying off.* He hopped up—and over onto my arm.

I braced myself against the stone to support his weight, not taking my eyes off his, afraid to breathe or blink. On my arm was a creature I had admired in books and in the sky for years. I had never known such awe. As I rose slowly to my feet, I felt something rub against the headstone. My jacket! In my excitement I'd forgotten to wrap it around my arm. But Red had balanced himself on the central, fleshy part of his feet, as though he knew not to hurt me. I took a few steps, trying to absorb everything about him.

He gave me a final look before he pushed off into the air. As he soared upward, I felt more than the weight of his body leave me. It was as if the knot deep inside me had loosened enough to release some of the grief and confusion that had grounded me. I watched Red until his bright plumage blended in with the sunrise. Then I stood beside Mom's grave for a long time, reliving those moments with Red.

I never saw Red again. He didn't come to the cemetery anymore, and I began going there less often. I started preparing for school and tuned back in to my family and friends. No, things would never be the same without Mom.

But the day Red perched on my arm, I saw something in his eyes that made the rest of my life seem worth living: God's promise that my future would always hold the wonder and joy my mother had wished for me.

The Tomato Patch

by Fran Younger Greathouse

OTHING WOULD GROW on the scarred land where the backhoe had dug up the earth on the far end of my property down by the creek. More than a year had passed since I had to put in a septic tank at my mountainside home, and I kept telling myself that it would take time for the ground to heal. The oak and hickory would reseed, the tiny acorns and nuts would sprout. But spring had come and gone, and all I could see from my dining-room window was a barren swath of brown earth and rocks. Even the wildflowers I had seeded didn't come up.

If my friend and neighbor Doris were alive, she would have been able to make something grow. On a warm day we loved to go down to the creek and watch the light play off the dancing water. Eventually, shadows would slip over the soft green hills. "I love this place just the way God made it," Doris would say in a near-whisper, "with things always growing."

In her garden, Doris grew lettuce, red cabbage, bell peppers, tomatoes. At the end of the previous summer—it seemed an eternity ago now—she brought me a big box of tomatoes. "Girl, there's every kind of tomato you could ever want," she said. More than I could ever eat. I had to dump the ones that spoiled down by the creek.

No one knew she was dying then. I certainly didn't. Sometimes she made excuses: "I'm just a little tired, Fran." She wouldn't go on a hike or a picnic. She wasn't outside in her garden as much. When I asked, she said she was getting over something. Nothing to worry about. Maybe if I'd known that was her last harvest, I would have canned all those tomatoes. I wouldn't have chosen to dig a septic tank. It could have waited.

The backhoe came the same month Doris died. My heart wrenched each time the powerful teeth grasped one of the young trees and ripped it from the ground. *Lord*, I prayed, *this is too much after the death of my friend*. To lose my wooded view and my neighbor all at once. I tried to imagine what Doris would say—that the land would heal, that God would bring it back more glorious than it had been before. "Just wait," I could almost hear her say.

I was tired of waiting. I wanted Doris to be here with me, to tell me the names of the birds I saw out my window and the critters rushing through the brush. I wanted Doris to bring me the bounty from her garden. I wanted to go on walks with her down by the creek. I wanted her here to comfort me, impossible as that was.

Then one morning I looked out my window and caught sight of a small red spot at the edge of the creek. *What's that?* I wondered. Had something blown onto my property? I put on my boots and went down to investigate. Not till I came to the edge of the bank did I see it—a tangle of tomato vines spilling across the ground. Right where I'd dumped those spoiled ones, the fruit of Doris's last crop. Every kind of tomato you could ever want. I felt Doris close to me. I could hear her saying in a near-whisper that even after a season of loss, God can heal—just as He makes dry land flourish again.

PART XII

Strength for Tomorrow

The Lord will give strength to His people;
The Lord will bless His people with peace.

Psalm 29:11 NKJV

TIME ITSELF MAY NOT HEAL BROKEN HEARTS, but it does change one's perspective. Think in terms of nature's seasonal adjustments: autumn, winter, spring, summer—each period evidencing its unique character, moving life forward. Most of the stories chosen here include a time element. They look back and show how God indeed gave strength not just on one day but strength that was renewed over time. The one exception might be "Riding Blind" by Cheryl Bransford. But in the end her outlook is so tomorrow-centered that it rounds out the theme. "I was learning how [to trust] again," she says. "It was the kind of trust we place in God when we have nowhere else to turn." May this section encourage you to trust in the God who "will give strength to His people."

Alone on the Farm

by Marsha Hedge

*T*HEY WERE SLEEPING SOUNDLY, both my girls. Too bad I couldn't say the same. I hadn't even changed out of my work boots. I slipped out of the house. Lately I'd been going for walks when I couldn't sleep. Tonight the summer moon cast a soft platinum glow on our rolling green fields, and I walked for a while, letting the stillness and the beauty ease the weariness in my bones.

My eyes fell to the spot by the end of our drive where my husband died. Had it been only a month? Dennis had been killed in a freak accident while using the four-wheeler to get around our farm. I felt a familiar stab in my heart and pulled my gaze away. Nothing could touch that ache. You love someone that much, one day without him seems like forever.

I went back inside. Time to get some rest. I had a long list of things to get done the next day. First, have breakfast with the girls; I wanted to keep their routine as normal as possible. Feed and water the cattle. In the afternoon, once the dew dried, I'd set to baling hay. My neighbors had offered to pitch in, but they had their own fields to worry about. Worrying. Farmers do a lot of that.

There was just so much to do on our 185 acres! Not that I wasn't used to country life. I grew up in Arkadelphia, Arkansas. Population: ten thousand. Living on a farm, where we could raise our girls to be self-sufficient, was our dream, Dennis's and mine. But being a full-time mom and part-time real-estate agent took most of my energy. Actually working the farm—Dennis had shouldered the bulk of that responsibility.

The place was a mess when we moved here. Dennis saw its potential, though. "We rebuild the fences, tend the pastures . . . it's going to make a nice little farm," he'd said. He pointed to a patch of grass out back, closer to the house. "We'll plant trees there so our kids can play in the shade. Our grandbabies, too, someday."

Sure enough, eight years and a lot of sweat—mostly Dennis's (he was a workaholic)—had turned that mess into a farm. A home. The only home our girls—Rachel, ten, and Kelsey, six—had ever really known. I'd lost my dad at an early age, and I remembered how my mom held our home, my brothers and sister and me, together, managing her school secretary's salary so wisely that we never felt we wanted for anything. That's why I'd instinctively dug in my heels when people assumed I would sell the farm.

For the girls, I reminded myself as I sank into bed that night. So they can have a connection, through the land. Yet the very next day I wondered. There I was, out in the middle of a field in the July heat, flat on my back under the hay baler, trying to untangle some twine that had wrapped around the machine's tines. How had my husband kept this farm running so smoothly—all the while working full-time as a veterinary medical officer for the Department of Agriculture too?

Fences, cattle, hay . . . I didn't worry, because Dennis took care of everything. His way. Capably. Meticulously. Perfectly.

A chunk of hay drifted into my eyes. I swatted it away. How could the Lord have taken Dennis from me? I was so angry at God, I couldn't even pray properly anymore. *Thanks, God,* I thought. *Now I do have to worry. About everything!*

"Marsha, you need a hand?" someone shouted. I wriggled out from under the baler. It was my nearest neighbor, the one who had shown me how to replace the belts in the mower and attach it to the tractor when I'd cut the hay three days ago. I was embarrassed he'd taken time out to come over again.

"Something's wrong with the twine motor," I told him. "That or the bale sensor." At least I'd gotten the terminology down.

"Hmm." He poked around the machine. "Yep, you're right on both counts. The computer chip on your bale sensor must be acting up. And the twine motor needs adjusting."

What next? I thought. *Is there anything else that can go wrong?*

"You look a little peaked, Marsha. You all right?"

"I'm okay," I said and turned the subject back to the baler. My neighbor agreed the baling would have to wait until I could get a repair tech to come out.

I made my way back to the house. I was so tired of depending on others. When would I learn to manage this place for myself? I collapsed in our living-room recliner. There, on the wall opposite, was my favorite picture of Dennis. My husband, wearing a ball cap studded with fishing lures, smiling at me. I would have broken down completely if I hadn't heard a soft voice. "Mama?" It was Kelsey. "I miss Daddy so much."

"Come here, Kelsey." I pulled her onto my lap. The next thing I knew Rachel was there too, touching my shoulder. I covered her hand with mine, remembering how my mom had comforted me after my dad died. How strong she'd been for me and my siblings. If I could only do the same for my daughters!

I swallowed my pride and asked neighbors to help with the baling. By the end of August, enough hay was cut, raked and baled to last our small forty-head herd through winter. Rachel and Kelsey were back in school, so I figured I'd return to real estate part-time.

Right. Except running the farm took so much time and energy that I couldn't add on showing properties and hope to have anything left for my daughters. There were fields to tend, cattle to feed and water, equipment and fences to maintain. Dawn to dusk, the chores were never-ending, even with the girls pitching in. Dennis and I had wanted to raise them to be self-sufficient, but it wasn't fair to ask them to take on more. Losing their dad was burden enough.

One Saturday they trooped along after me in the tangy fall air to fix fences. Rachel held the posts steady while I hammered. Kelsey was my gofer, fetching nails, tools and water. Tough way for two kids to spend a Saturday, but I didn't hear a single grumble. We finally finished. "We didn't do too bad, huh?" Rachel asked. Kelsey looked up at me proudly.

"Not bad at all," I said, throwing an arm around each of them as we walked slowly to the house. "We make a pretty good team."

I took a last glance back at the fence. To me, the section we'd repaired stood out, the cross-braces looking not quite so perfectly straight as the ones Dennis had put up. *I'm sorry*, I wanted to tell him. *No matter how hard we try, we can't do things right, the way you did.*

The months and the grief wore on. I got stuck in the mud driving around our rain-sodden fields to check on the cows. That winter I took over Dennis's job of keeping the stock pond from freezing over. The cattle had to drink, so I broke up the ice with an ax three times a day, leaving me wet and chilled to the bone. Sure, a less stubborn woman would have given up. But I had to keep going. For the girls.

I must have sounded as miserable as I felt, because Mom took to calling every couple of days. She would claim she just wanted to say hi, chat with her granddaughters since the dreary weather was keeping them cooped up inside. But she was checking on me. "Marsha, I've been meaning to tell you something," she said one day. "You've done a really good job keeping things going. I'm proud of you."

"I haven't done anything nearly as well as I should have," I said. "Not like you. How did you manage so well on your own?" She hadn't had much education or money, after all.

Mom was quiet for a moment. Then she said, "I wasn't on my own. I had help." She paused. "Marsha, only God could help me find the strength to do things my way. Without Him, I don't know what I would have done. Accepting His help was the only real choice I had."

I considered that long after we hung up. I'd thought certain people, like my husband and my mother, were naturally more capable, with some inner resolve that went deeper than what the rest of us had. It hadn't occurred to me that strength might come from another source: the One whom I'd been so angry at for taking Dennis and leaving me to fend for myself.

God, You helped Mom. Help me. It was such a relief to ask that. I could almost hear Dennis chuckle somewhere up there in farmers' heaven and say, "Now you've got it, Marsha."

Once you turn to God, turning to others doesn't seem so hard. Come spring, I asked a neighbor to show me how to hook up the tractor equipment again. I snapped pictures of each step so I wouldn't forget.

And I haven't. I'm still working the farm. A local crew does the haying for a share of the bales. I had a freeze-proof drinking fountain installed for the cows. Rachel, Kelsey and I have become even more proficient at building fences. Good thing, too, since we've added another 120 acres.

I used to think I was staying on here for the girls, the memory of their father, the legacy of the land. True. But I'm also staying for me. I look out back now, and I see the trees Dennis and I planted, growing, thriving. Just like our dream. One day I'll walk our grandkids under the shade of those trees and show them around the farm, show them why there's no place on God's green earth I'd rather be. And with a little help, this is where I'll stay.

Butterfly Lady of Swinney Switch

by Bethany Homeyer

ERHAPS IT WAS MEANT TO BE. For my son's funeral, a photo of a monarch butterfly was chosen for the cover of the program. Michael had lost his life at eighteen in an auto accident, and in my grief I clung to the hope of that image: the butterfly rising triumphantly from the chrysalis. A symbol of Christ's own promise of life after death.

And yet, in the weeks after the funeral, I found little comfort or reassurance. I dragged myself through daily life —fixing dinner, doing the laundry, driving to the post office—and then sank into despair. The smallest thing would set me off: a vision of Michael running down the path through the garden or stooping to pick a caterpillar off a leaf, each memory a deep ache in my soul.

Michael was my "nature child." He'd bring home insects, presenting them to me as though they were trophies. I'd stand there admiring the ladybugs he held in his chubby hand. "Be careful," he'd say as I leaned close. "Don't hurt them." He might keep them in a shoe box for a day or so, but he always released them back to nature to be free.

Once, after washing his overalls, I discovered a bunch of pill bugs in the pockets.

"Look!" I showed the bugs to Michael. "They survived the wash!" We marveled at the hardiness of God's creatures, and let them go in the garden.

Now I kept asking God the impossible: Why couldn't Michael have survived the accident? Why couldn't He bring my son back to me?

The only thing that kept returning to me was the image of that butterfly—a golden monarch fluttering across a clear blue sky, alighting on a flower. In the months after Michael's death, I found myself irresistibly drawn to information about butterflies. I read books, looked for courses I could take, spoke with lepidopterists. Was God sending me this passion to fill the hollow space in my heart?

Tens of thousands of species of butterfly live on every continent of the globe. They fly by day, sleep at night and come in a dazzling variety: The coppery queen lives on milkweed; the black-and-yellow giant swallowtail drinks citrus nectar; the gorgeous ebony-and-yellow mourning cloak feeds on wildflowers. In my studies, I felt close to Michael. He would have been fascinated. Sometimes I glanced up from a book and thought he was there, reading over my shoulder. Sometimes I talked to him as if he were still with me.

In time I began to see the study of butterflies not so

much as a way to escape my grief but to embrace it—to honor Michael's memory by doing something he would have loved. *I'll raise butterflies,* I decided.

We had the perfect place, a lakeside garden in our temperate Texas climate. I had always been interested in organic gardening, and we had plenty of trees and shrubs to produce leaves that would feed the caterpillars. I contacted a breeder, bought some larvae and put them in shoe box-size containers lined with paper towels and leaves. Day by day I watched the caterpillars grow until they formed their chrysalides. Then came the moment when they slowly emerged and unfurled their wings. When they took flight, the sky above my garden was filled with color, as though flowers had taken to the air.

That first summer of raising butterflies brought one joy after another. I felt Michael near me, the way he had been at my side as we watched bees buzz from flower to flower. Released from my sorrow, I wanted to share this beauty with others. I kept thinking about all the milestones that Michael would never reach: graduation from college, his wedding, the birth of his first child. And then I had an idea: Why couldn't I start a business offering butterflies for such occasions? To celebrate beauty, joy and freedom. Michael's Fluttering Wings, I called it. He would have liked that. With the help of some friends, I launched the company.

Since we started Michael's Fluttering Wings, we have

provided thousands of butterflies to fill the gardens and skies at countless events. We take great care of our butterflies, feeding them in their boxes and then keeping them in a large netted cage with plentiful nectar. I am incredibly thankful for this business, the way it lifted me out of my grief and showed me how to move from mourning Michael to honoring him. Yet it was not an overnight process.

Not long ago I was reading about an experiment done by the great English biologist Alfred Russel Wallace. Observing an emperor butterfly struggling to leave its chrysalis, he wondered what would happen if he helped the process along. He slit open the chrysalis with a knife. But, as he wrote, "The butterfly emerged, spread its wings, drooped perceptibly and died." Without the pain and intensity of the struggle to get free, Wallace concluded, the butterfly lacked the strength necessary to survive.

I thought of how I came through the grief of losing my son. It was a long, at times agonizing, struggle, and yet in it I found the strength to go on, to accept the wings God offered.

Riding Blind

by Cheryl Bransford

*I*N OCTOBER 1981, MY HUSBAND GORDON died suddenly. Against everyone's advice, I took over his business, Meadow Creek Outfitters, which outfitted and escorted hunters into the Selway Bitterroot Wilderness area, a prime game area in Idaho's Nez Perce National Forest. I was a young mother with four children, and I needed that business to keep my family fed and clothed.

But it was a rough year. There were hunters still on the trail when Gordon died, and others were booked for the season. My two oldest children, Tara, twelve, and Josh, seven, were in school, and the two youngest, Tyler, four, and Colter, one, needed full-time attention at home. There were bills to pay, letters to write, and laundry, groceries and cleaning to take care of. Equipment had to be repaired, staff had to be hired, animals had to be tended, and hunters had to be transported back and forth from the airport in Lewiston, seventy miles away. The children's grief over Gordon's death had to be lived through. And there was my own sadness. I felt lost without Gordon.

I felt overwhelmed, and sometimes I wondered if I shouldn't listen to those well-meaning advisers who told me, "Outfitting isn't a woman's job. Take your kids and go back to your folks in Oregon."

Then came that dark autumn night a year after Gordon's death. It was an unforgettable night.

For the first hunt of the season, I had joined the rest of the staff in Otter Butte Camp to help with the full two weeks. It was a busy time, and I was doing everything I could think of to make things go smoothly: cutting firewood, saddling the horses each morning, feeding and watering the animals each night, helping with the cooking. But one morning toward the end of the first week, I heard the men grumbling. We were running low on eggs, and Sharsty, the cook, had not served them with breakfast.

"You expect us to eat these pancakes without eggs?" everyone complained. "This ain't a decent breakfast," one of them griped. "We'll be starving in an hour!"

That made me so darned angry that I saddled up Duly, my horse, took one of the pack mules, and yelled over my shoulder to Sharsty, "I'm riding into town for supplies."

"You're what?" She looked startled.

Still stinging from the insinuations behind those complaints—that a woman couldn't handle this business—I headed down the trail. It was a four-hour ride over rough terrain and then a hundred-mile drive over mountain roads to Kooskia in my rig. By the time I bought groceries, loaded up the pack mule and started back for camp, it was evening. Only then, with night setting in, I realized how foolhardy I'd been.

The trail ahead was perilous: a two-hour ride down into a deep ravine, and then a two-hour ride that wound up onto Otter Butte. I was afraid. How could I possibly find the way?

As Duly and the pack mule and I started the descent, I wondered if I shouldn't turn back, go back home where it was safe. I was in the dark; I'd been afraid of it all of my life. And now, here I was alone, terrified, in the blackness of this wilderness.

Winding slowly down into the darkness reminded me of the dark days following Gordon's death, when life seemed so impossible. Being alone, dealing with the children's grief that festered into tears and temper tantrums, making all of the decisions on my own—those days were nerve-racking, just as this night was, full of unseen challenges, rocks and holes, cliffs that I somehow had to maneuver.

The farther down I descended, the more despair I felt. I had taken on a responsibility too big for me. I could never manage this business and give my children the kind of life they deserved. "I should be home with them right now, instead of leaving them at the neighbor's," I chided myself. "Why didn't I go back to my folks in Oregon?"

It was a moonless night, and I was riding blind. I blamed myself for riding like this into the wilderness alone. I was not that familiar with the trail. What if Duly slipped? What if the pack mule shied and dragged me? That's what caused Gordon's death. The pack mule had dragged him, had torn off two of his fingers, and days later Gordon had died of gangrene.

I heard something. I strained to listen. It was water, water rushing over rocks. We were near Otter Creek. I could feel Duly picking his way slowly down, and then I heard the splash as his hooves hit the water. We were at the bottom. As the animals lumbered across, I had to make a decision.

This is where the trail splits. The trail I wanted led on up the cliff and into camp. The other was used by animals coming to the river to drink.

My sense of direction had gone with the darkness, but I turned Duly onto the trail I thought led to camp. He refused to move. A cold clamminess overtook me. "Come on, Duly," I urged, but Duly didn't budge. Swinging out of the saddle, I tried to lead Duly up the trail. I tugged. I pleaded. I yelled. I cursed the darkness that hid the way.

And then I did something that I hadn't done since Gordon died. I began to trust. "All right," I said to Duly. "You win." I placed myself in Duly's care because I had no other choice. Back in the saddle, I held the reins loosely and gave him a nudge. Duly had traveled this trail many times with Gordon. He had night vision. He knew the way better than I.

As my horse turned and headed up the other trail, steadily, surely, I felt relief. The worries, the despair and self-blame lifted. I clung to Duly and let him carry me up the winding, narrow way.

For all of those long, miserable months I had not been able to trust anybody. But now, on Duly's back, I was learning how again. It was the kind of trust we place in God when we have nowhere else to turn, when we have no other choice, when our despair is so great that we give up and say, "Okay, God, I'm lost. You lead the way." Who knows? Perhaps that was God's little lesson for me.

As Duly and the pack mule and I made the two-hour climb into camp, my spirits rose. *I will make a go of this business*, I told myself. *My kids are going to be fine! They're going to survive, and so am I. We'll live and grow in this wilderness, and nothing, nothing will defeat us.*

And the next morning, you should have seen those hunters grinning over the scrambled eggs on their plates!

How Will I Go On?

by Dolia Gonzalez

GENTLE GULF BREEZE blew in as Secretary of the Navy John Dalton escorted me to a seat next to the dais on the main deck. It was October 12, 1996, and hundreds of people had gathered at the naval station in Corpus Christi, Texas, to witness the commissioning of the USS *Gonzalez*.

I thought I was past tears, but my eyes began to fill as an officer spoke about the ship's namesake: my son, Freddy. A Marine sergeant, he had run through heavy fire to help an injured man in Hue City, Vietnam, in February 1968. Wounded in the rescue, Freddy refused treatment and stayed with his squad. A few days later, they were positioned in an abandoned building when Freddy spotted an enemy sniper taking aim at two of his men. He pushed them to safety, but took a bullet and was killed instantly.

For twenty-one years my son had been the center of my world, and it had taken me a long time to get over losing him. As the speaker continued recounting Freddy's achievements, memories flooded my mind.

My husband had left me before Freddy was born, so at

home, at church, on the way to school, it was always just the two of us—my son and me. It wasn't easy living on what I made as a waitress in a diner, but we managed. Even as a little boy, Freddy did his best to help. Despite my protests, when he was only ten, he insisted on finding a job. I'll never forget the afternoon he returned, jeans and T-shirt caked with grime, holding his first pay from picking melons. "Here's some money for groceries, Mom," he said, his smile as big as Texas.

As Freddy got older, he spent summers toiling in the cotton fields, never complaining about the back-breaking work or keeping a cent of what he earned for himself. On Saturdays he sometimes asked shyly, "Mom, some of the kids are going to the movies, and I was wondering if. . . ."

"Go ahead, Freddy," I'd urge. "Have a good time!"

The spring of his senior year, Freddy started coming home from school ravenous. He ate everything that was on the kitchen counter and then cleaned his plate at supper-time. I figured he must be going through another growth spurt. Then one evening Freddy gave me a big hug and handed me a small velvet box. Inside was a beautiful pin— a dainty porcelain rose trimmed with gold. "What is this for?" I asked, stunned.

"Mom, it's Mother's Day. I wanted you to have something nice."

The look on his face melted my heart. I was even more

touched when his friends let it slip that Freddy hadn't bought lunch for two months to save for my gift. No wonder he had been so hungry.

Freddy joined the Marines right out of high school. I tried to tell him we would find a way for him to go to college, but he wouldn't hear of it. "Mom, I don't want you to worry about college," he said. "We'll be able to afford it after I'm out."

To fill the lonely evenings while he was away at boot camp, I started thinking about the future. Maybe, after Freddy was done with the service and with college, we could get a house. Freddy was excited when I told him about my plans. "That's a great idea, Mom!" he said. "Just wait. Someday I'll build you a place on Sugar Road." It was a pretty area on the outskirts of town. I had no doubt that one day we would be living there in our own house, because Freddy had a way of making things happen.

Shortly thereafter, he shipped out to Vietnam. Though he wrote every week, telling me not to worry, I lit candles and prayed constantly. Freddy made it back safely, but when he learned some of his buddies had been killed in action, he volunteered for a second tour of duty. "I owe it to the guys," he told me, his voice as serious as I had ever heard it.

A terrible fear began to overtake me after I didn't hear from him for two weeks in February 1968. One morning I went to the diner early because I couldn't sleep. When I glanced out the window and saw a Marine in full dress uniform getting out of a car, I knew.

"Hero . . . courage . . . sacrificed. . . ." I heard the officer's words, but I couldn't react. In a daze, I let the man drive me home. The apartment floor seemed spongy, as if I could sink into it. I wanted to sink down somewhere, anywhere, to get away from this place Freddy and I had shared for so many years, this place where he would never return.

After Freddy's burial with full military honors, I stayed home from work for an entire month, hardly able to get out of bed. When I finally trudged to the diner, I almost wished I hadn't. Most of my customers had known my son and offered their condolences. Though I appreciated their sympathy, each mention of Freddy was an awful reminder that he was gone.

Except for visiting his grave, I spent my nonworking hours sleeping. Nothing had meaning for me without Freddy: not friends, not family, not even life itself. I barely ate and lost twenty-five pounds. On Sundays I couldn't bring myself to go to church, knowing I would have to sit in the pew alone.

Work, cry, sleep. Month after month slipped by as I remained mired in a profound depression. I lost awareness of everything except Freddy's absence and the constant raw ache in my heart. My faith, which had always carried me through difficulties before, failed to lift me. I tried to pray, but invariably I ended up wondering, *Freddy was so good. Why did he have to die, God? Why?*

Only two things brought me the slightest comfort during that dark time. The first was when Freddy was posthumously awarded the Medal of Honor, the Purple Heart and the Vietnam Service Medal with two bronze stars. The second was something one of Freddy's favorite teachers told me. When she saw she was getting nowhere trying to console me, she finally asked, "Dolia, when you go into a garden, don't you try to pick the best flowers?" I nodded. Then, squeezing my hand, she said quietly, "Maybe God also takes the best."

Still I clung to Freddy's memory, unable to pull myself together and move on. Then one night seven years after his death, my son came to me in a dream. He was a teenager again, full of life, happiness dancing in his eyes. He walked toward me through a field so lush with flowers that he appeared to be swimming through them.

"Don't worry, Mom," he assured me with a smile. "I'm fine." Before I could reply, he turned to leave. A path in the flowers opened up as if to guide the way. I reached for him, desperately wanting to go along. Freddy looked back at me and waved good-bye. I ran after him, but I couldn't catch up.

When I awoke, I felt a peace in my heart that I hadn't

known since Freddy died. And I understood immediately what my dream had meant. Though Freddy's life was over, I still had mine to live. *Thank You, Lord, for sending my son to me one last time. And for realizing I couldn't get over his loss without Your help.*

At the diner that morning, when one of my regulars ordered the usual, I teased, "Why don't you put some spice in your life and have the French toast for a change?"

He looked at me quizzically. "Dolia, you're smiling!"

"I guess I am," I replied, and I found myself smiling some more. I started going to church again, and I finally took my friends' advice and joined a counseling group for bereaved parents. It felt good to be connected to the world again.

Not long after, the mayor called and told me the Board of Education had voted to name the new elementary school after Freddy. "It's not far from you," he said. "On Sugar Road."

I nearly gasped, recalling my son's long-ago promise. He had built me a place on Sugar Road after all—the Freddy Gonzalez Elementary School, which has become my second home. I go there every morning to drop my nephew off for classes, and I help in the lunchroom three days a week. I've gotten to know most of the kids. When new students wonder who I am, I tell them, "Do you know the name of your school? Well, I'm Freddy's mom."

Nearly twenty years after Freddy's death, the Navy

informed me they planned to name a ship after him, an honor reserved for a distinguished few. As I sat on the deck of the USS *Gonzalez* at the commissioning ceremony, I realized it no longer made me sad to say I was Freddy's mom. My son's life may have been short, but it was special. *Lord*, I thought, *maybe one day I'll understand why You took Freddy. For now I'm proud—and grateful—You made me his mom.*

The officer next to me whispered, "It's time, Mrs. Gonzalez." I took a moment to compose myself and then I walked to the dais. I looked at the ranks of sailors standing at attention. Taking a deep breath, I called out, "Officers and crew of the *Gonzalez*, man the ship and bring her to life!"

With bells ringing, horns tooting and sailors swarming to their stations, the ship came to life. And I said a prayer of thanks that, in a quieter but no less dramatic way, God had helped me do the same.

PART XIII

Hope of Heaven

Whom have I in heaven but You?
And there is none upon earth that I desire besides You.
My flesh and my heart fail;
But God is the strength of my heart
and my portion forever.

Psalm 73:25–26 NKJV

IS THERE A HEAVEN? What is it like? Who will be there? . . .
Some of our after-death questions won't be definitively
answered in this life. And yet . . . Scripture itself gives us
clues. "There are no tears in heaven," as Pat LaGrone was
reminded in a sympathy letter that had more significance
than its sender would ever know. And now and then we
find people who have seen visions, dreamt scenes, or
stepped to the edge of death and looked beyond. They're
like Nikki McFaul, who describes a garden landscape and
comments, "If only there could be a place like that!" Read
on, and though your questions won't all be answered, be
assured that your hope of heaven is founded and sure.

The Letter

by Pat LaGrone

BEFORE THE PARTY STARTED, I hoped to steal upstairs to the trunk where I kept our son Rod's favorite things. I spent a lot of time with that trunk since Rod's death in a car accident in his sophomore year in high school. That's where I went when I missed him so much I couldn't bear it. Like now.

My husband Rodney and I had decided to throw a graduation party for Rod's classmates. They'd taken his death hard too. In the months after the accident, the kids wrote dozens of letters telling us how much our son had meant to them, how they'd never forget him, how they were praying for us. I saved every one and packed all of them away in a box for safekeeping. Throughout their junior and senior years, the kids dropped by the house just to say hi or talk about Rod. Sometimes I'd almost forget that he wasn't right out front, shooting hoops in the driveway.

The soda was on ice, the chips and dip were out. Rodney was firing up the grill. "I'll be down in a few minutes," I called to him. I hurried upstairs to the trunk, which I'd found in an antiques store about six months after Rod's death. I went through Rod's treasured possessions one by one, savoring each memory as I packed them neatly inside. His freshman yearbook, his Latin Club scrapbook, his Star Wars action figures. Each time I went through the trunk, I repacked it just as carefully, laying the University of Alabama football quilt I'd had made for him on top before closing the lid.

Our first guests would arrive any minute. I opened up the trunk and frowned. The quilt was there as usual, but there was a letter on top of it, one we received after Rod's death. It wasn't like me to leave a stray one out. Those letters were too precious to me. I always kept them bundled together in a separate box up in my closet. And nobody went into the trunk but me.

I checked the signature on the letter. Rod's friend, Hugh Biggs. I was disappointed when Hugh told me previous plans would keep him from making our party. The doorbell rang downstairs. I smoothed the quilt and closed the trunk, tucking the letter into my pocket. I'd put it back in its proper place as soon as I had a chance.

The kids were full of talk about their class rings, college plans and career dreams. They looked so happy. I put out the desserts and slipped into the bathroom, hoping no one had noticed my teary eyes. *God, help me to remember that Rod is eternally happy with You.*

I leaned against the closed door and pulled Hugh's letter out of my pocket. "Why all these tears?" he wrote. "We are crying because we miss Rod, but Rod is happier than he ever was on earth, because he is with God. There are no tears in heaven." I'd forgotten what Hugh had written. Or perhaps I wasn't ready to take it in two years ago. But tonight I took his words to heart.

Thank You, God. This misplaced letter was a blessing today.

The next morning I put the letter by the phone to remind myself to call Hugh and tell him how much his words had meant to me, two years later—if under somewhat mysterious circumstances. I was finishing up the dishes when the phone rang. It was my neighbor. "Did you hear about Hugh Biggs?" She sounded upset.

I picked up the letter. "What?" I asked quickly, a prayer for Hugh already on my lips.

"He was killed in a car accident."

All I could think of was Betty, Hugh's mother. I knew her pain. My pain. A pain no words could ease. Still I felt like I needed to go to her.

I slipped Hugh's letter into my purse. An angel put this letter out to ease my pain. *Please, God, help me find the words to ease Betty's pain.*

Her husband Clyde met me at the door. "I'm so sorry," I said. Clyde nodded sadly, his shoulders slumped. Looking at him brought back those awful days right after Rod's death, when it didn't seem like anything would ever be all right again. No kind words helped me then. How could I expect my own words to mean anything to Betty now? Maybe I should have waited to come.

"How is Betty?" I asked.

Clyde rubbed his face. "I don't know what to do." He hesitated, like he wasn't sure if he should go on. I nodded encouragement. "We went to the funeral home," he said. "Hugh was crying." Clyde shook his head. "The mortician said it was normal, just the tear ducts emptying, but it looked so real. Betty feels like Hugh is crying somewhere, and she can't comfort him." Clyde ran his hands through his hair. "How can I help her?"

The letter in my purse! There are no tears in heaven. Hugh had written those words himself. "Let me talk to her," I said.

Betty was in the bedroom, lying on her side. "Pat," she said weakly, her eyes red and swollen.

I sat next to her and put the letter into her hand. "Hugh wrote this after Rod died. I was reminded of it yesterday when I needed its soothing message. Today, I believe, these words are meant especially for you."

Betty read the letter. It was a long time before she could speak. "Do you really believe Hugh is happy, like Rod? That he isn't crying?"

"An angel put this letter in our hands," I said. "God must have wanted us to know it's the truth."

I put my arms around Betty. We would never really stop hurting over the loss of our boys. But God had found a way to ease our pain today. Tomorrow He would find another way. And then another. Until we were with our boys in heaven, and our tears were left behind for good.

The Promise

by Nikki McFaul

THE FIRST TIME I SAW GLORIA MARSHALL, she was singing in the choir at Fairview Community Church. My six-year-old son Colin pointed her out. "Mommy, there's my Sunday school teacher," he said. She was a small-framed woman with wispy brown hair haloing her face. And when she sang, her face purely glowed.

My husband, four children and I were newcomers at the church, and ever since we'd joined, Colin had been raving about his teacher. I patted his hand, grateful he liked her, thankful my kids were able to have the kind of Christian experience that had been missing in my own childhood.

While my mother was a traditional Christian, my father was not. They were divorced, and I'd lived with my mother, brother and sister in a little duplex in California. As the choir sang that Sunday morning, I recalled those days vividly, especially the year I was eight. That was when Mama got cancer. We had a picture of Jesus on our living-room wall, and sometimes Mama would look at it and say that if she died, Jesus would take her to heaven, where she would watch over us.

One night I awoke to find Mama bending over the double bed where all of us children were sleeping. I watched dreamlike as she kissed each of us. The next morning she was gone. She'd been taken to the hospital, where she died that same day. She was forty years old. I thought about what Mama had said, that she would go to heaven and watch over us. More than anything, I wanted assurance that it was true.

I went to live with my father. He didn't believe Mama was in heaven. He explained that her soul had gone to sleep. Period. With time and tutoring, I came to believe as he did, that death was an ending, that there was no consciousness, just the mist of eternal slumber.

That's pretty much the idea I'd lived with all my life. Then a few years ago, I found a deeper, personal relationship with Jesus Christ. Now I was trying to believe in God's beautiful promise of eternal life. But to be honest, it was difficult sometimes to put those deeply ingrained doubts behind me.

After the service at church that Sunday morning, I made a point to meet Colin's teacher. Gloria Marshall was a single parent with three children; she worked at a center for mentally handicapped children. As we talked, I had the compelling feeling that she was someone I should get to know better.

In the weeks to come, however, I saw her only occasionally at church functions. Then one December afternoon, I plopped into a dining-room chair to read the church newsletter. Inside was a note from Gloria thanking the church for supporting her as she faced a recurrence of her cancer. Cancer? Why, I didn't even know she was sick!

As I sat there, Tiger, our old tabby, slinked over and purred against my leg. I rubbed the cat's ear, a sudden idea nibbling in my thoughts. In my work as a stress counselor, I often used positive mental imagery to help clients find healing. Maybe Gloria would consider working with me, no charge.

She was more than willing, and we began therapy sessions in January, meeting weekly in my office and at home. Gloria and I experimented with various meditations and visualizations that would help her envision God's love and healing being released into her life. Inviting a healing image into the mind can have a powerful effect on the body, and Gloria and I kept searching for the one just right for her.

One day as we began our session, a unique, imaginative image popped into my head. "Close your eyes, Gloria," I told her. "Call up a picture of a winged horse." As she followed my direction, I said, "Imagine that he has been sent to you by God, and he can fly you anywhere you choose to go. Now climb on his back and let him take you to your own special healing place."

Maybe it was whimsical, but when Gloria opened her eyes after a few minutes, she was more relaxed than I'd ever seen her. "Oh, Nikki," she cried. "He took me to the most beautiful garden, where I walked and talked with Christ. There were flowers and springs of water."

The winged-horse meditation became her favorite. Again and again she would travel to the imaginative garden to meet the reality of Christ's presence. During her communion she often pictured Jesus giving her "living water" from the springs along the garden paths.

As spring came and went, a bond of closeness formed between us. Best of all, Gloria improved. An exam showed her inoperable tumor was actually shrinking. "Whatever you're doing, keep doing it," her doctor said. And we did.

Meanwhile, Colin's attachment to Gloria deepened too. She became his most beloved babysitter. One weekend, Gloria kept Colin so that my husband and I could get away for some time together. When we returned, Colin was quieter than usual. That night I tucked him in bed, planting a kiss on his forehead.

"Mommy, what will happen to Gloria if she dies?" he asked.

"Gloria will live in heaven with Jesus," I answered, hoping he did not sense the uncertainty in my voice.

Colin closed his eyes, but the little frown of worry remained on his face.

Gloria had been progressing for six months when the change began. Gradually I noticed her energy waning. She grew thinner. Soon the doctor confirmed my fear: The tumor was growing again.

Before long, Gloria was unable to go on with our sessions. At our last one, she presented me with a ceramic figure she'd made herself, a pastel blue horse. A winged horse.

"I will not give up hope, but I have to face the possibility I may die," she told me. "Perhaps the healing garden in my meditation is really heaven." She said it with such peaceful simplicity that I thought my heart would break.

"No—" I protested.

Gloria knew I struggled with doubts about the hereafter, and she interrupted me, a twinkling light in her eyes. "When I die, I'm going to be your best guardian angel, Nikki. I'll still be around. You'll see."

Autumn arrived. I threw myself into a busy schedule. I called Gloria often. Her voice seemed weak, like a sound fading in my ear. But while the leaves turned loose and drifted away, Gloria held on.

It was during the Christmas Eve service at church that I discovered her condition had suddenly worsened. After church, I hurried to her house. Gloria's bed was surrounded with people speaking in hushed tones. "She's in a coma," her mother told me.

I lifted Gloria's hand into mine. "It's Nikki," I said. "I'm here. I love you." Her eyelids flickered. For a moment she seemed on the verge of speaking; then she lapsed back into her comatose sleep. I squeezed her hand and left. Outside, Christmas tree lights flickered in windows along the street. I knew I would not see Gloria again.

At home I retreated into my office, feeling desolate. Oddly the pain of losing Gloria kept mingling with memories of my mother. I remembered that my mother had died at the same age Gloria was now, of the very same disease.

Oh, Gloria.... I picked up the ceramic winged horse from my desk, thinking of the garden she had visited in her meditations. If only there could be a place like that!

Gloria died early Christmas morning. During the late afternoon, we attended her memorial service at the church. Gloria had requested we sing the French carol "Angels We Have Heard on High." But even when we sang the chorus, "Gloria in excelsis Deo," setting Gloria's name to angelic music, I could find little peace.

Later I stood before my bedroom window. The night was cold and starry. I gazed into the darkness for a long while; then I went to bed, exhausted.

In the wee hours of the morning, I awoke from a deep sleep, strangely alert. I cannot begin to explain what happened next. I simply felt what I thought to be the cat sink onto the foot of the bed against my feet. Tiger knew good and well she was not allowed on the bed. I moved my foot to nudge her to the floor, but she was not there. Then I remembered: I had put Tiger outside for the night.

I peered through the shadows. Nothing at all was on my bed, but the weight remained! It pressed against my feet, unmistakably, gently.

Suddenly a peculiar warmth glowed in the room as if it were enveloped by an electric blanket. My friend Gloria was there. I knew it. The certainty of it seemed indisputable to me.

I do not know how long I lay there with the mysterious pressure on the foot of my bed, but I had the overwhelming feeling that any moment I might actually see her sitting there.

Gradually, though, the weight on the bed disappeared. As it did, my mind was seized by a mental picture, like a movie playing on a screen inside my head. I saw Gloria in white, walking through a garden of unspeakable beauty, a garden blooming with bright flowers and flowing with streams of silver water. I saw her reach out her hand to a shining figure I knew was Christ.

The image faded. I drifted into tranquil sleep.

When the alarm buzzed some hours later, the room was harsh with sunlight. I climbed from the bed, trying to come to grips with the experience of the night before. In the cold light of day, my intellect wanted a rational explanation. How could such a thing have happened? Was it some imagined illusion? Or had Gloria actually reached across the gulf to give me the assurance I needed so desperately in my life?

Bewildered, I wandered into the hallway. There I bumped into Colin, hurrying from his bedroom. His face was lit with wonder, with that special look a child gets when he sees something wonderful for the very first time.

"Mommy," he said, "why was Gloria sitting on my bed last night smiling at me?"

I gazed into his small upturned face, transfixed. Precisely at that moment I remembered Gloria's words: "When I die, I am going to be your best guardian angel. I'll still be around; you'll see."

I took Colin in my arms. "Perhaps Gloria came to assure you she is fine," I said full of certainty.

I still marvel at the glimpse of another reality that God granted to Colin and me that Christmas. I don't know why it happened. I only know I found the assurance I had longed for all my life: that death is merely a portal into another dimension, a heavenly dimension that, like the garden in Gloria's meditation, brims with beauty and life and the radiant presence of Christ.

A Sweet Taste of Heaven

by Sue Foshee

DENISE LOVED WATERMELON. As a little girl, she couldn't get enough of it come June. Her father and I always had to keep an eye on her and those sticky black seeds. Denise was known to spit them at her brother and sister when we weren't looking. "Denise!" I'd scold when I caught her in the act. Denise would giggle and flash her trademark grin.

At sixteen, Denise had lost none of her mischievousness. Not even when she was diagnosed with cancer. She had a kidney removed and then radiation treatment. My heart broke, but through it all Denise put up a brave front. The cancer came back, and exploratory surgery was our next course of action. I dreaded what it might reveal. "I'm not afraid," Denise kept insisting. "I know God is with me."

As playful and fun-loving as Denise was, she had a deep, serious faith. We went together to the revival at our church just before her surgery. I hoped the visiting minister would have fresh words of reassurance for us.

Denise and I sat down and the minister took the podium. He let a moment of silence go by before he began. "I don't know exactly what heaven will be like," he said.

"But there's one thing I'm sure has got to be there." He looked from person to person. "Watermelon!" he said with delight. "Sweet, juicy watermelon, fresh from the patch. When I get to heaven, I'm going to have as much watermelon as I want." Everybody laughed.

Denise nudged me with her elbow. "Me too," she whispered. She gave me that grin. I frowned at the minister. Maybe he could make jokes about heaven, but I couldn't. Not with us so unsure about the state of Denise's health. Besides, heaven was a place to rest after a long, full life. Heaven was peaceful and serene. It was no place for a girl who still turned cartwheels out on our front lawn. *God, she's so full of joy. Please don't take that from her.* I had to force myself to sit through the rest of the meeting.

When Denise's father and I took her to the hospital, we didn't talk about heaven. We stuck to happier subjects. What we would do when Denise was better, the new football team at the high school, and the garden I was planning for the yard. Jack and I settled into her room. "We'll be here when you wake up," I told Denise as the orderly wheeled her away.

"I know, Mom," she said, her grin wide even now.

After the surgery was over, the doctor met us in his office. Our worst fears had come true. The cancer had spread to Denise's spinal cord. It was too far advanced to treat. "You may be able to take her home in a few days," the doctor told us, "but she won't have much time after that."

I moved as if in a fog to Denise's hospital room, where she was still sleeping off the anesthesia. I looked at her face, trying to memorize it forever, all the details, down to her pierced ears. That's what she'd wanted for her sixteenth birthday. We went down to the mall and picked out her first pair of earrings, small pink gems. Could it really have been only seven months ago? *God, I don't know if I can ever begin to accept what's going to happen.* I couldn't even think it.

Slowly Denise came to, groggy at first. I sat with her into the night. We talked about little things. She dozed on and off. "You're really going to start a garden, Mom?" she asked. I nodded, swallowing my tears. Denise would never see it bloom. I tried to picture her at peace high above the clouds. But that didn't seem like my Denise! Denise played jokes, did somersaults, spit watermelon seeds. Would she be different in heaven? Would I even recognize her?

Denise's gaze wandered through the room, but she was quiet. "Mom?" she said finally. "Do you see the angels?"

I looked around. "What do they look like?" I asked.

Denise's face softened into her sweet, playful grin. "Really pretty."

It was strange to think Denise was seeing God's glorious angels and grinning like a girl who'd just gotten her brother right smack on the cheek with a watermelon seed. Then I remembered that minister, how he described heaven as a place full of joy and life, full of watermelon. Maybe he was onto something, after all.

Denise didn't mention her angels again. She grew weaker and weaker over the next twenty-four hours. We never got to bring her home. She died in the hospital three days after her surgery. It was springtime, the perfect time to start a garden. I got as far as spreading soil, but my heart wasn't in the job.

One morning, I stood looking at the rich, fresh dirt. I imagined how the bed would look in full bloom. Hostas and ferns, perhaps. Impatiens of all colors. A garden bursting with life. Just like that lively heaven the minister had described. I wanted to believe that place existed. I tried to picture Denise laughing and joking as she'd done on earth. I was about to walk away when I noticed a thick green vine half hidden in the soil. Jack and the kids didn't know what to make of it. We decided to wait and see what grew. Over the next few days, leaves appeared and light yellow flowers bloomed on the vine. *I didn't plant this*, I thought to myself when football-shaped melons showed themselves. Not just any melons, but the biggest, brightest watermelons I had ever seen.

We cut one open one night after they'd ripened and each had a slice. I reached for seconds, knowing somewhere in heaven Denise was probably joining us—and gaily spitting seeds at the angels. Why shouldn't heaven be full of joy and laughter? How could it not be, with Denise there?

Table for Two

by Alisa Bair

M Y SIX-YEAR-OLD DAUGHTER Kelly and I were walking hand in hand down the street, on our way to get milk from a nearby convenience store, when she finally asked the question. I had anticipated it. I knew it had to come sooner or later, and I hoped I was ready for it.

"Mommy, could I die from this?" she asked, her clear sweet voice wrenching my heart on that warm July afternoon.

Three weeks before, Kelly had been operated on to remove a malignant brain tumor. She was about to begin months of radiation and chemotherapy. Our family of five floundered for mooring in a sea of physical and emotional turbulence.

Lauren and Leslie, fourteen and eleven, tried hard to balance the desperation they sensed in my husband Rob and me by making it their mission to try to buoy the spirits of their younger sister. They sang songs and played games with her, distracting her from crankiness during painful procedures. Knowing Kelly sorely missed Tucker, our one-year-old sheltie, they brushed the pup until they had collected enough fur to bring to the hospital for her to hold lovingly against her cheek.

But in spite of the cheerful caring from them and many others, I knew it was inevitable that someday Kelly would connect the words *cancer* and *death*.

"Some people die of cancer, but many do not," I began carefully, grateful to be walking beside her and not having to be face-to-face, where she would surely see my eyes reddening and ask again, as she had done countless times in her hospital room, "Mommy, are you crying?" I couldn't bear the concern my tears caused her. "They removed all your tumor and you'll be getting treatment," I said. "That means you have a really good chance of living a long, long life."

"I'm not afraid of dying, because I know I'll be with Jesus," she said. "I'm just afraid of how I might die."

I wanted to shelter her with great wings, like a mother bird over her young. But instead I now had to help Kelly trust her own wings.

"I don't think dying hurts too much," I said, "because the nurses and doctors can give you medicine to help you. We would be right there, holding you, and it would be just like we passed you into the arms of Jesus."

She continued, her voice more fervent than before: "I don't want to be the first in our family to die."

Her words stung, and I struggled to sound matter-of-fact: "Any one of us could die first. Anyway, for the person who's in heaven, it probably only seems like seconds till she sees her family again."

After six weeks of intensive radiation, we began to adapt to the new routine of hospitalizations, chemotherapy, blood counts, transfusions and MRIs at the Children's Hospital in Philadelphia. One bitterly cold day in January, we drove out of the hospital parking lot. Kelly was curled under a blanket pulled up to her nose, her voice muffled inside her woolen cocoon: "You didn't forget, did you, that I want to be baptized?"

That had been her persistent question as we went through several church changes in recent years, and more recently after her diagnosis. "Did you ask Pastor Tom if I could be, uh . . . you know, baptized like you were?"

"You mean immersed?"

"Yeah, immersed."

Pastor Tom Fries set the date for April 4, Palm Sunday. We held a private service that was attended only by family and a few close friends. Kelly chose a brand-new white hat to wear for the occasion.

As we tucked her into bed that night, we complimented her on her poise and reverent attitude toward the sacrament. "Not many people take this as seriously as you did today," Rob told her. "God must really be pleased."

One morning in late June, as I settled down to a cup of tea at the kitchen table, hoping for a quiet hour before the girls woke, I heard the top step creak.

"Mommy," came Kelly's voice as she rounded the bottom of the stairway.

I turned, surprised to see her out of bed, her beloved worn teddy bear dangling from her hand. "What are you doing up so early?"

"I had the best dream," she said, touching my arm to make sure she had my full attention. "I dreamed I was with Jesus."

"How did you know it was Jesus?" I asked, intrigued.

"I just knew," she responded. "We were eating together."

"Where?" I asked.

She paused and then said with great tenderness, "At a table for two."

Table for two? Has she ever heard the term before? "What were you eating?"

"I don't remember any food, but I know we were eating." She said other people were dining nearby, but her table was bathed in light. "Oh, Mommy," she said. "I feel so close to God!"

Kelly's dream comforted me and gave me hope—but not, I would soon discover, for the reasons I had thought.

In August, on the day of yet another routine MRI, two weeks after Kelly's eighth birthday, the phone rang. "Mrs. Bair? This is Dr. Molloy. . . . You might want to sit down. . . ." The cancer had recurred. Kelly did not have much time left.

On a crisp September evening five weeks later, Pastor Tom looked out over a sanctuary brimming with family and friends who had gathered for Kelly's memorial service. Sobered by the grief around them, Kelly's young classmates sat quietly with their parents.

"*You prepare a table before me in the presence of my enemies,*" Pastor Tom read from Psalm 23 NKJV. "Kelly's enemy was cancer, and she saw, in a dream, the table God had prepared for her."

During the service, Lauren and Leslie reenacted Kelly's dream, which she had described to us in more detail. They draped a purple tablecloth over a small table flanked by two chairs and set it with two white dinner plates and a single lit candle.

Months later, Rob took a day off so we could sort through Kelly's things. Slowly, painfully, we emptied her shelves and bureau drawers and packed books, toys and clothing in boxes—some to give away, some to keep. We reminisced, pausing for tears when we needed to.

Finally, the floor vacuumed and the room stripped of its comfortable clutter, I looked at the red crayon scribbles I had once scolded Kelly for making on the white lamp shade on her bedside table.

The bedside table. "Rob," I said, sighing, "we forgot to empty this." I opened the drawer, which was crammed full of small toys, tablets, markers and trinkets. I sorted through them and then lifted out what lay at the bottom: a notebook. I opened it, hoping to see a drawing, spelling words, anything.

Inside was a surprise. Kelly had kept several journals throughout her illness, but here was one we hadn't seen— empty except for two entries, dated shortly after she had had her dream.

It was as if we were reading a letter from her in her new residence. Here, using her exact words and spelling, is what she wrote:

Dear Jesus,

I really felt much closer to you these past years, and I still do. I have felt your presents more. I thank you for this time of cancer through the past year and a-half. It has given me a time to get even closer to you! I am so excited to come to your kingdom someday! I don't know anything about what heaven looks like, I know it's going to be the best place I have ever been! It feels so good to know that I'm in your arms, safe and sound! I couldn't of goten through last year without you, Jesus!!!

. . . This year I really feel like one of God's mitionaris. I feel a messag to tell people about God! It's a very, very, very neat and special feeling. . . .

Rob and I held each other and wept. Kelly had found the secret of rejoicing in her suffering. Her voice seemed to say, "You can too, Mommy and Daddy."

Reading her words, I was filled with an intense longing to know more fully the beauty of the holiness she saw and tasted. It had caused her to bask in the joyful intimacy of friendship with God. It had made her want to reach out with the good news of redemptive hope. I thought of a note we received from a young girl at the memorial service: "Dear Kelly," it read in childish scrawl. "Enjoy your supper with God."

Supper with God, I thought, taking the chair Jesus seemed to be holding out for me—at my own table for two.

Nothing to Hide

by Deb Sistare

I WAS FIFTEEN WHEN MY DAD DIED, and Mom took our family to live with Grandma and Grandpa. They were a perfect pair of opposites. She was short and plump; he was tall and skinny. She had a head full of wild white hair; he had a thin band of fuzz from ear to ear. She was always in high gear; he walked with an easy shuffle. Grandma went to church on Sundays; Grandpa didn't. "Why doesn't Grandpa go with us?" I finally asked my mother one Sunday while we were getting ready.

"He just doesn't," Mom said. "And you shouldn't ask such personal questions of people. It's just not polite." I hadn't meant to be hurtful. I loved Grandpa. After school I'd stop off at his barbershop and watch him cut hair in his careful, deliberate way. On warm summer evenings, we'd sit under the pecan tree, and Grandpa would teach me life lessons. "If you borrow money and say you'll pay it back Friday morning, then do it," he said. "Even if you have to borrow it again on Friday night." Some nights, when Grandpa fell asleep in his old lounge chair, I'd put on red lipstick and kiss him on his bald head. When he woke up and came into the kitchen, Grandma would burst out laughing.

"What's so funny?" Grandpa would ask, two red lips standing out on his shiny head. Then he'd see me struggling to keep a straight face and go to the mirror, knowing I'd gotten him again.

Much as I became Grandpa's shadow, though, some things remained a mystery. Like why did Grandpa smell of cherry pipe tobacco during the week and on the weekends smell like whiskey? Plus, I'd seen his name on the church roll. Why had he stopped going?

One weekend I found Grandma frantically pulling towels out of the closet in the bathroom. "Did you lose something?" I asked. Grandma shook her head and stuffed a few more towels under her arm. "There it is," she said, sounding relieved. She held an unmarked bottle of amber liquid I knew was whiskey. As I watched, Grandma poured a trickle down the drain of the chipped porcelain sink. "If I empty it, he'll just buy another bottle," she explained as she added water. "So I dilute it a little at a time. By tomorrow, he'll be sober enough to go to work." Grandma put the bottle back in the closet. "I can't let him lose the barbershop." Without asking any questions, I handed her the towels, one by one, until everything was back in its place.

I watched Grandpa closely that week but didn't notice anything unusual until Friday night. I smelled whiskey on him. When we got back from church on Sunday afternoon, he was dozing in his easy chair. *He doesn't look drunk*, I thought. But when he got up and walked past me, eyes downcast, he didn't smile. His feet dragged like lead weights across the floor and into the bathroom.

I went to find my mother. She was reading in her bedroom. "What is it, Deb?" Mom asked. I hesitated.

"Is Grandpa okay?" I managed finally.

"Sure," Mom said, her tone clipped. "He's just tired. He worked hard all week." She went back to her book. *Grandpa's just tired*, I repeated to myself. Then I heard Grandma wrestling with the towels in the bathroom closet and went to help her. She stacked them in my outstretched arms. Grandpa must have been ashamed of his drinking, I figured, and that's why he tried to hide it from Grandma. *Maybe that's why he doesn't go to church anymore. He wants to hide from God.* Like the week before, Grandma stuck the bottle under the faucet without a word.

After a while, our Sunday routine seemed almost normal. Almost. Grandpa remained the same loving man, and he continued to be "tired" on the weekends. I grew up and moved out on my own, but I visited my family regularly.

When I was thirty, Grandpa was diagnosed with terminal cancer. I spent a lot of time sitting beside his bed, talking to him. The whiskey bottle was never far away now. *He's too sick to hide it anymore*, I thought one night as I watched him sleep. Grandpa had spent too much of his life trying to keep his problem from us and from God. The worst part was that we had helped him do it.

"You should have asked God for help," I whispered to Grandpa, kissing his bald head. "We all should have."

Then I had an awful thought: If Grandpa's secret had kept him from church, could it keep him out of heaven as well? *Please, God, forgive us all. And take my grandpa into heaven.*

After Grandpa died, the thought continued to haunt me. One night I had a strange dream. Grandpa was standing at the bottom of a steep, pearl-white staircase that reached way into the clouds. He gazed up at a huge angel who held out a satiny, emerald-colored robe, open and waiting, it seemed, for Grandpa himself. When Grandpa headed up the stairs, he wasn't shuffling. At the top of the stairs, the angel helped Grandpa into the robe and tied the sash so the rich folds of material fell around him. Then the angel took Grandpa's hand, and together they disappeared into the clouds.

The picture of Grandpa wrapped in that shiny emerald green robe was fresh in my mind when I met Grandma for lunch the next day.

Grandma was adjusting slowly to life without Grandpa. "I miss him terribly," she admitted. "He was a good man. Even though he had a drinking problem."

I couldn't believe she had said it openly. "Yes," I said, "he did have a drinking problem." It was a relief to admit it aloud. But Grandma looked frightened.

"He didn't go to church," she said. "I don't know if he asked God's forgiveness. I'm so afraid he didn't go to heaven!"

I wrapped my arms around Grandma, feeling closer to her than I ever had in all the years I'd lived in her house. The secret that had always stood between us was gone. "Last night I dreamed about Grandpa," I said. Grandma sat very still and listened. When I got to the part where Grandpa slipped into the green robe, her eyes filled with tears. "He made it, Deb," she said. "He really made it."

"But, Grandma, it was just a dream."

Grandma shook her head. "Let me tell you something," she said. An expression came over her face that I'd never seen before. "Something we never told anybody else. One Sunday at church when we were first married, your grandpa saw an angel standing right on the altar. He said that angel was at least ten feet tall, standing right behind the preacher and smiling down at him during the service. And your grandpa said that angel was wearing the most beautiful green robe—'a robe that glistened like emeralds' were the words he used. 'When I get to heaven,' he said, 'I want a green robe just like the one that angel was wearing.' What else could that dream be but a sign from God that Grandpa is with Him?"

What else, indeed. God sees our weaknesses, and He loves us despite them. I believe He has an angel with an emerald green robe waiting to welcome each of us, flaws and all.